PROPHETIC INSIGHTS FOR DAILY LIVING

VOLUME 2

~~

Inspired Messages From The Holy Spirit

Sheila Eismann

Books by Sheila Eismann

A STORMY YEAR – BOOK 2 OF THE SABBLONTI SERIES

A WOMAN OF SUBSTANCE – A 12-WEEK BIBLE STUDY

CREATIVE AUTHORS' WORKBOOK JOURNAL – A STEP-BY-STEP GUIDE FOR YOUR WRITING EXPERIENCE

HEART TO HEART FROM GOD'S WORD

LOVE, THE TIE THAT BINDS – BOOK 3 OF THE SABBLONTI SERIES

JANTZI'S JOKERS – BOOK 1 OF THE SABBLONTI SERIES

POETRY TIME – VOLUME ONE

PROPHETIC INSIGHTS FOR DAILY LIVING – MESSAGES INSPIRED BY THE HOLY SPIRIT – VOLUME 1

PROPHETIC INSIGHTS FOR DAILY LIVING – MESSAGES INSPIRED BY THE HOLY SPIRIT – VOLUME 2

PROPHETIC INSIGHTS FOR DAILY LIVING – MESSAGES INSPIRED BY THE HOLY SPIRIT – VOLUME 3

RECOGNIZE YOUR CIRCLES

STIRRINGS OF THE SPIRIT

STRAIGHT FROM THE HORSE'S TROUGH

THE CHRISTMAS TIN

Copyright © 2021 by Sheila Eismann.

www.sheilaeismann.com

All rights reserved. No portion of this book may be reproduced, stored in a retrieval system, or transmitted in any form or by any means — electronic, mechanical, photocopy, recording, scanning, or other — except for brief quotations in critical reviews or articles, without the prior written permission of the publisher.

Published by Desert Sage Press
www.desertsagepress.com

Printed and bound in the United States of America.

Cover design by Cathie Richardson. **www.countrygardenstitchery.com**
All rights reserved.

Any trademarks, service marks, product names, or named features are used only for reference, are assumed to be the property of their respective owners, and the use of any one of those terms does not imply an endorsement on the part of the author and/or the publisher.

ISBN: 978-1-7373135-1-9

Library of Congress Control Number: 2021913577

Scriptures are taken from the New King James Version. Copyright 1979, 1980, 1982 by Thomas Nelson, Inc. Used by permission. All rights reserved.

Scripture quotations marked (NIV) are taken from the Holy Bible, New International Version®, NIV®. Copyright © 1973, 1978, 1984, 2011 by Biblica, Inc.® Used by permission of Zondervan. All rights reserved worldwide. www.zondervan.com. The "NIV" and "New International Version" are trademarks registered in the United States Patent and Trademark Office by Biblica, Inc.®

DEDICATION

This series of workbooks is dedicated to my beloved husband, Dan, who our precious grandkiddos affectionately refer to as "Poppy." He's my best friend, confidant, loyal companion, and fellow believer in our Lord and Savior, Jesus Christ. I will be forever grateful for God knitting our hearts together in His love and giving us compatible and mutually beneficial spiritual giftings.

We've experienced challenges, supreme blessings, miracles, and victories during the 38 years of our marriage. God has sustained us every single day and step of the way by His mighty right hand, His beloved Son, Jesus Christ, The Holy Spirit, His Word, and His ministering angels.

We're eternally grateful for all of the divine appointments God has orchestrated with those of His choosing throughout the intersections of our lives.

It's been the honor and privilege of a lifetime to walk side-by-side with Dan as we continue to learn, laugh, and love together. To God be the glory, both now and forever more!

ACKNOWLEDGEMENTS

My heartfelt gratitude, sincere appreciation, and blessings are extended to Cathie Richardson, Lesta Chadez, and Marilyn Battisti for their invaluable assistance and encouragement in publishing this set of prophetic workbooks.

It's been a special joy to share this experience with my oldest daughter, Cathie, whose artistic gifts and talents bless me beyond measure. For a real treat, please check out her website: **www.countrygardenstitchery.com**

Fifty-three years ago, Lesta and I lived in the same small rural area. Our paths reconnected at just the right time. Despite navigating her own set of life's challenges, Lesta's dynamic combination of mercy and exhortation is a bonus for any writer. In addition, she's a poet, author, and spiritual song writer.

Being a retired school teacher, Marilyn operates from a unique vantage point concerning almost everything she reads and studies, especially as it relates to spiritual matters. I continue to be amazed when reading her thoughts if she opts to post a comment on my website after I've authored one of my blog posts! Since Marilyn has a real heart for intercessory prayer, she's blessed my life immensely as a prayer partner.

In addition, I want to thank my Lord Jesus for helping me every day in every way. With Him, all things are possible. (Matthew 19:26) I'm grateful for The Holy Spirit and His gifts of creativity which are inherent within each of us in various forms.

TABLE OF CONTENTS

Introduction 13

The New Year's Dream: The Maze & The Kiss 27

The Open Gate 39

The Sea, The Bottle & The Scroll 49

Prophetic Vision: A Blank, Bank Check 59

Prophetic Vision: Hot-Off-The Press 71

During February: Tweak Your Wheelhouses 80

The Maturity Is In The Waiting 90

The Time Of Your Life 102

A Cup Of Joy 114

Where Is Your Car Parked? 117

Going Your Own Way 125

Prophetic Dream – Preferential Treatment 135

The Woman, The Wishing Well & 1932 144

An Eruption Of Miracles 154

Knitting Together God's Plans 163

Double Divine Justice - The Blindfolds Are Suddenly Removed! 172

Beneficial Boundaries 180

Strength, Dignity & Laughter In Our Immediate Future 186

The Seed Bag, The New Field & The Scarecrow 194

Ride & Decree Victory! 204

About The Author 213

Other Books Available from Sheila Eismann, Dan Eismann & Desert Sage Press 215

Notes and Reflections 220

FOREWARD

Woven into the fabric of our lives wherein a silver cord is intertwined throughout the tapestry, there are people in our circle of friends where our hearts are bound together through the Holy Spirit. Sheila Eismann is a special friend that God has placed in my life as the Lord has knit our hearts together in His love. We grew up in the same rural town, and our parents were friends. From this friendship, a bond of love was birthed.

As I have read Sheila's books and followed her writings and blogs over the years, her prophetic visions and dreams have ministered to me in many areas. I give praise to our Lord and Savior Jesus Christ for the many ways He has been with me throughout my life. The Lord especially filled my heart with a living hope through a time of testing when my husband entered into his eternal home in 2019. Special friends like Sheila prayed for me through this difficult journey, and I will be forever grateful for the many ways the Lord has strengthened me and given me hope.

Sheila has a gifting and unique way of weaving in words of wisdom, encouragement, and exhortation as she shares with us what the Lord has given her in visions, dreams, and prophetic words. When we face times of trouble, testing, or tribulation, she has a way of bringing her messages to a practical application in our daily lives by sharing words of comfort and hope while challenging us to pursue a deeper walk with the Lord.

The prophetic visions and dreams the Lord has shared with Sheila are for anyone who wants a fresh infusion of faith and strength to start each day. They are for those walking through difficult seasons of life such as loneliness, grief, or change. The wisdom the Lord shares with her may be for those who are overwhelmed by life's challenges and for those who may be concerned about loved ones or the condition of the world around us. When it seems like the circumstances of life and the storms that surround us are pulling us under, she reminds us that the Lord is the Victor and encourages us to continue to put our trust and hope in Him as He is faithful and true to His promises and His Holy Word.

Every day we need wisdom and fresh insight as we walk out the fullness of our salvation in our journey through this earthly life. The workbooks that Sheila has prepared can be a devotional and also used in a Bible study. Her prophetic writings will be a blessing to those who have open hearts ready to receive what the Lord has for them.

Lesta Chadez, Poet, Spiritual Song Writer, and Author of *Treasures Hidden In Plain Sight, A Collection of Poems and Short Stories.*

You will be ever so blessed to read the prophetic articles by Sheila Eismann. Each of her visions is a timely message to guide and direct you in your everyday living. Having the inspiration from The Holy Spirit, each of Sheila's writings is a direct appointment for you to individually meet with our Lord Jesus and find manna for your soul. Sheila's prophetic visions will definitely inspire you and lift you to another level of Christianity!

Marilyn Battisti, Retired Educator

INTRODUCTION

Prophetic Insights For Daily Living was written with you, the spiritual seeker, Bible reader, and student, in mind to render assistance regarding spiritual gifts, dreams, visions, and prophetic words.

To introduce this new series of workbooks, I deem it's important to go into greater detail concerning the three revelatory gifts of the Holy Spirit listed in 1 Corinthians 12:4-11. These gifts are the word of wisdom, the word of knowledge and discerning of spirits.

"There are diversities of gifts, but the same Spirit. There are differences of ministries, but the same Lord. And there are diversities of activities, but it is the same God who works all in all. But the manifestation of the Spirit is given to each one for the profit *of all:* **for to one is given the word of wisdom through the Spirit, to another the word of knowledge through the same Spirit**, to another faith by the same Spirit, to another gifts of healings by the same Spirit, to another the working of miracles, to another prophecy, **to another discerning of spirits**, to another *different* kinds of tongues, to another the interpretation of tongues. But one and the same Spirit works all these things, distributing to each one individually as He wills." [Emphasis mine]

Writing to the church at Corinth, Paul said, "Now concerning spiritual *gifts*, brethren, I do not want you to be ignorant:" [1 Corinthians 12:1]

During its establishment phase, God did not want the church in Corinth to be ignorant concerning these matters, and His desire is no less for present-day churches or Bible-believing Christians.

An important aspect to remember is the Holy Spirit distributes His gifts to each one individually as He wills. [1 Corinthians 12:11] Every single one of the spiritual gifts outlined in 1 Corinthians 12:4-10 is precisely just that, a gift which cannot be bought, traded, manufactured, contrived, manipulated, or you fill in the blank.

<u>The Holy Spirit gift of the word of wisdom and the gift of the word of knowledge:</u>

"Before we begin our study of the gifts of the Holy Spirit, it is important for us to understand that in the scriptures there is a mingling of gifts, so much so that at times we may question just which gift (or gifts) is being manifested. This need cause us no real concern, for it must be remembered that all of the gifts flow from the same source, The Holy Spirit. If we are unable to identify exactly and classify perfectly, let us not be overly concerned. As humans, it is our nature to draw neat lines of separation and classification, but when we seek to impose this practice upon God, we only frustrate ourselves, and we may generate unnecessary confusion.

The word of wisdom and the word of knowledge are two gifts that often work together. Throughout the Old Testament when the prophets would prophesy, the word of wisdom and the word of knowledge would flow together (knowledge, and what to do about it.) In reading the prophetic books of the Old Testament, you will notice the phrase time and time again, "The WORD of the Lord came to _____ (name)." Examples of this can be found in 1 Kings 17:8; Jeremiah 1:4-8; Ezekiel 1:3; Joel 1:1 and Haggai 1:1.

In the New Testament, much of the writings of Paul, Peter, James, and Jude are the word of wisdom and word of knowledge. Also, John's letters to the churches in Revelation chapters 2-3 are this mixture. The word of wisdom often comes with the word of knowledge so that believers in Christ will know how to apply that knowledge correctly. These gifts are two of the three gifts that 'reveal' something. We call these gifts revelation gifts because they consist of information supernaturally revealed from God. Each of these gifts is the God-given ability to receive from Him facts concerning something, anything, about which it is humanly impossible for us to know, revealed to the believer so that he or she may be protected, pray more effectively, or help someone in need.

The gift of the word of knowledge is supernatural in character. It is not obtained by logic, or deduction, reasoning, etc., or by natural senses, but by supernatural revelation through The Holy Spirit. It is the sheer gift of God. It is not essentially a vocal gift. It is received quietly and inaudibly within the person's spirit. It may become vocal when shared with others.

A basic definition of the word of knowledge: a fragment or small item of God's knowledge, supernaturally revealed to a person by The Holy Spirit.

An example of a spoken word of knowledge can be found in John 1:47-49:

'Jesus saw Nathanael coming toward Him, and said of him, 'Behold, an Israelite indeed, in whom is no deceit!'

Nathanael said to Him, 'How do You know me?'

Jesus answered and said to him, 'Before Philip called you, when you were under the fig tree, I saw you.'

Nathanael answered and said to Him, 'Rabbi, You are the Son of God! You are the King of Israel!'

It is important to consider what the word of knowledge is not:

- It is not human knowledge gained by natural means.

- It is not human knowledge sanctified by God.

- It cannot be gained by intellectual learning, studying books, or pursuing academics.

- It is not the ability to study, understand, or interpret the Bible.

- It is not a psychic phenomenon or extra-sensory perception such as telepathy (the supposed ability to be able to read minds), clairvoyance (the supposed ability to know things that are happening elsewhere), or precognition (the supposed ability to know the future.)

The gifts of the Spirit defy human scientific explanation and are not acquired by ordinary educational processes. No amount of education or learning can produce them. They are not dependent upon innate human qualities. For example, the word of wisdom might be spoken by a person of even less than ordinary wisdom. They are not accentuated natural talents and abilities. The least talented or able may as likely be the agent through whom God works as the most intellectually endowed.

It is a subtle ploy of the great deceiver of our souls to attempt to humanize the supernatural and to reduce the spiritual gifts to the level of mere human endowments, talents, and learned or acquired abilities.

A word of knowledge may be revealed to a believer in any of the following ways:

- A sudden inspiration or a deep inner impression.

- A dream, vision, or picture seen through the eye of the spirit, with the interpretation of what is seen.

- Hearing the voice of God, or of angels, audibly or in the ear of the spirit.

- A living personal word from the Lord through scripture.

- The vocal gifts of the Holy Spirit such as tongues, interpretation of tongues, or prophecy. [1 Corinthians 12:10]

Supernatural visions and dreams are usually the word of wisdom or word of knowledge in operation. Acts 2:17-18 reminds us of what was spoken by the prophet Joel,

> *'And it shall come to pass in the last days, says God,*
> *That I will pour out of My Spirit on all flesh;*
> *Your sons and your daughters shall prophesy,*
> *Your young men shall see visions,*
> *Your old men shall dream dreams.*
> *And on My menservants and on My maidservants*
> *I will pour out My Spirit in those days;*
> *And they shall prophesy.'*

The word of knowledge may not always be fully understood by the receiver or the hearers. It can seem like it's a riddle or a mystery. In the seventh and eighth chapters of the book of Daniel, we read where the prophet was troubled in his spirit, and the visions that were given to him disturbed him greatly. In Daniel 8:27b, God's servant was appalled by the vision, and it was beyond his understanding.

Oftentimes God will use a word of knowledge to uncover sin, bring people to Him, give guidance and direction, minister encouragement, or impart knowledge of future events. Some Bible scholars teach the revelation of future events to be the gift of the word of wisdom rather than the word of knowledge since wisdom usually pertains to what to do in the future.

If you would like to take the time to examine some examples of a word of knowledge in the Bible, I have listed a few from the Old Testament and the New Testament.

Old Testament:

- 1 Samuel 3:10-14
- 1 Samuel 10:17-23
- 1 Kings 19:11-18
- 2 Kings 5:20-27
- 2 Kings 6:8-23

New Testament:

- Luke 2:25-26

- John 1:29-34
- John 6:60-61
- John 13:38
- Acts 5:1-11

Hosea 4:6a reminds us that God's people are destroyed for lack of knowledge. We definitely need the gift of the word of knowledge operating in our lives and churches today!

The word of wisdom is a flash of inspiration. It is a supernatural revelation sufficient for the occasion of the wisdom or purpose of God. It is the wisdom needed to meet a particular situation, or answer a particular question, or utilize a particular piece of information.

Once again, it is vital to consider what the word of wisdom is and is not:

- It is not natural wisdom.
- It is not the wisdom gained from academic achievement.
- It is not wisdom gained from experience.
- It is not even the wisdom to understand the Bible.
- It is given as the Holy Spirit wills (1 Corinthians 12:11).
- It is given for a specific need or situation.

A word of wisdom may be revealed to a believer in Christ the same way that I have listed previously for the word of knowledge.

It is helpful to know that we can pray for wisdom, understanding, and knowledge. In Ephesians 1:17, Paul prayed for the spirit of wisdom and revelation. In Colossians 1:9, Paul asked God to fill the believers in the church in Colosse with the knowledge of His will in all wisdom and spiritual understanding.

The following are examples of a word of wisdom found in the Old Testament and the New Testament:

Old Testament:

- Genesis 6:13-21

- Genesis 41:33 with Acts 7:10
- Exodus 28:3; 31:6 and 35:26
- Judges 7:5
- 2 Samuel 5:17-25

New Testament:

- Matthew 2:12-15
- Matthew 21:23-27
- Luke 20:22-26
- John 8:3-7
- Acts 27:23-26[i]

The Holy Spirit gift of discerning of spirits:

"The third gift along with the word of wisdom and word of knowledge that reveals something is the gift of discerning of spirits. It has a narrower range than the other two because it is limited to the spirit world.

Sometimes this gift has been called the gift of discernment which is in error. It is the gift of discerning of spirits. It is not the gift of discerning people; it is the gift of discerning of spirits. There is a huge difference.

From our study of scripture, we learn that there are four basic categories of spirits in the spirit world which are as follows:

- God - John 4:24
- Angels – Hebrews 1:14
- Evil spirits, deceiving spirits and demons - Ephesians 6:12; 1 Timothy 4:1 and Revelation 16:14
- Man - Zechariah 12:1; 1 Corinthians 2:11a

A believer in Christ may be (1) operating under the inspiration of the Holy Spirit; or (2) expressing his or her own thoughts, feelings, and desires from his or her soul or spirit; or (3) allowing an alien spirit to oppress him or her and be bringing thoughts from that wrong spirit. An unbeliever in Christ may be completely possessed by an evil spirit. (Luke 8:26-39) The gift of discerning of spirits immediately reveals what is taking place. This gift is given to know what is in a person and to know the spirit that motivates him or her.

First, we need to define the word 'discern.' It is looking beyond the outward to the inward, literally, 'seeing right through', or 'insight.' In the gift of discerning of spirits, it means to distinguish between good and evil spiritual influences.

The following three verses are a sample of how the word 'discern' is used in the Bible:

- 2 Samuel 14:17 – 'And now your servant [the woman from Tekoa] says, 'May the word of my lord the king bring me rest, for my lord the king is like an angel of God in discerning good and evil. May the LORD your God be with you.' [NIV]

- 2 Samuel 19:35a – 'I [Barzillai the Gileadite] *am* today eighty years old. Can I discern between the good and bad?'

- Ezekiel 44:23 – 'And they [the priests] shall teach My people *the difference* between the holy and the unholy, and cause them to discern between the unclean and the clean.'

Some Biblical scholars believe that if there are no visions, (actually **seeing** the spirit), it is not the gift of discerning of spirits, but rather the gift of the word of knowledge in operation. They reason that if one is informed about a spirit, but has no vision of the spirit, he or she would not **discern** it. In some cases, a WORD comes first, then a vision follows.

Through the gift of discerning of spirits, we can discern the origin of certain actions, teachings, and circumstances that have been inspired by spiritual beings. It is the ability given by God to know what spirit is motivating a person or situation. The gift allows a believer to detect and identify spirits and provides supernatural revelation of the unseen spirit world, both good and evil. The real nature of this gift is knowing and judging – never guessing.

The gift of discerning of spirits is not a natural critical spirit, insight into human nature, human shrewdness, character reading, fault-finding, psychological insight, or even spiritual discernment. It is not a spiritual gift to uncover human failings. It is not the spirits of people who have died. It has nothing to do with spiritism or spiritualism. The spirits of departed human beings are not on this earth and to attempt to contact them is forbidden. [Deuteronomy 18:9-12]

Discerning of spirits is needed primarily to reveal the source of spirits. The first and most obvious function of this gift is to reveal the presence of evil spirits in the lives of people or churches. However, it also functions to evaluate the source of a prophetic message, a particular teaching, or some supernatural manifestation. The person functioning with this gift will be able to tell whether the source of the message or act is demonic, divine, or merely human. The gift of discerning of spirits enables a Christian to pick out the source of gifts and messages that truly come from God. Humans cannot be in contact with or understand the spiritual realm except by the power of God or the power of Satan. (1 Corinthians 2:14)

Although the gift has to do primarily with evil spirits, it also is the ability to detect the presence of the Holy Spirit. Visions, seeing Jesus or angels are also included in the discerning of spirits. If one only discerns evil spirits, then the Holy Spirit gift of discerning of spirits is not in operation.

Our natural discernment can be easily fooled. The gift of discerning of spirits is a means of protection from satanic deception. It is easy to confuse the words of the spirit of Satan with those of the Spirit of God. Satan counterfeits the beautiful works of God by creating an outward appearance that is similar to the real work of the Holy Spirit.

Satan is known as the deceiver [Revelation 12:9], the father of lies [John 8:44], and the serpent [Revelation 20:2]. All these titles signify the subtle, crafty deceptiveness which he uses to bring about evil whenever he can. Many times, his counterfeit is so plausible that one will be entirely deceived unless someone is present who functions with the supernatural gift of discerning of spirits. If demon activity was always so obviously reeking with evil and wicked intent, as we tend to imagine, there would no use for this gift of the Holy Spirit."[ii]

The following are examples of discerning of spirits found in the Old Testament and the New Testament:

Old Testament:

- Genesis 21:17-19

- Leviticus 19:31

- Deuteronomy 32:17

- Judges 13:3-7

- 1 Samuel 16:14-15, 23
- 1 Samuel 28:11-19
- 1 Kings 19:5-8
- 2 Kings 6:17
- 2 Chronicles 18:18-22
- Zechariah 3:1-2

New Testament:

- Matthew 1:20-21
- Matthew 16:23
- Luke 1:11-20; 26-38
- Luke 13:11, 16
- Acts 12:7-10
- Acts 13:9-11
- Acts 27:23-24
- 1 John 4:1"

Despite teachings to the contrary, God's people do receive dreams, visions, and prophetic words today. Here's a basic overview of this aspect of the revelatory realm:

1. God communicates through His prophets in one of two ways. "Let the prophet who has a dream tell the dream, but let him who has my word speak my word faithfully."[iii] As an aside, why would God want to stop communicating to us through prophets? Has He stopped speaking? Do people no longer need to hear from Him?

2. *Nābiy'* prophet. One of the ways God communicates to us is through a *nābiy'* prophet. "This word describes one who was raised up by God and, as such, could only proclaim that which the Lord gave him to say. A prophet could not contradict the Law of the Lord or speak from his own mind or heart."[iv] "I [God] will raise up for them a prophet [*nāḇiy'*] like you [Moses] from among their brothers. And I will put my words in his mouth, and he shall speak to them all that I command him."[v] Jeremiah was a *nāḇiy'* prophet, and he tried to refrain from giving the word of the Lord because doing so made him "a reproach and derision all day long."[vi] However, he could not refrain from giving the word of God.

> If I say, "I will not mention him,
>   or speak any more in his name,"
> there is in my heart as it were a burning fire
>   shut up in my bones,
> and I am weary with holding it in,
>   and I cannot.[vii]

3. *Hōzeh* prophets. Another way that God communicates to us is through a *hōzeh* or *chōzeh* prophet (hereinafter *hōzeh* prophet). "The word is "[a] masculine noun meaning a seer, prophet. . . . The word means one who sees or perceives; it is used in parallel with the participle of the verb that means literally to see, to perceive. . . . It appears that the participles of *hōzeh* and *rā'āh* function synonymously. But, terminology aside, a seer functioned the same as a prophet, who was moved by God and had divinely given insight."[viii] *Rā'āh* or *rō'eh* is "a verb meaning to see" and can "connote a spiritual observation and comprehension by means of seeing visions."[ix]

A prophet can function as both a *nāḇiy'* prophet and a *hōzeh* prophet. For example, Jeremiah functioned as both.

> But the Lord said to me,
>   "Do not say, 'I am only a youth';
>   for to all to whom I send you, you shall go,
>   and whatever I command you, you shall speak.
>   . . . .
>   declares the Lord."
> Then the Lord put forth His hand and touched my mouth, and the Lord said to me:
>   "Behold, I have put My words in your mouth.
>   . . . .
>   And the word of the Lord came to me, saying, "Jeremiah, what do you see?" And I said, "I see an almond branch." Then the Lord said to me, "You have seen well, for I am watching over my word to perform it."[x]

King David was assigned all three types of prophets.

> Now the acts of King David, from first to last, are written in the Chronicles of Samuel the seer [*rā'āh*], and in the Chronicles of Nathan the

prophet [nā<u>b</u>iy'], and in the Chronicles of Gad the seer [hōzeh], with accounts of all his rule and his might and of the circumstances that came upon him and upon Israel and upon all the kingdoms of the countries.[xi]

4. Examples of the ministry of prophets include the following:

a. Rebuking someone for sin.
The LORD sent Nathan the prophet to David to tell him a story about a rich man who stole and prepared for eating a lamb that had been raised in the home of a poor man.[xii]

Then David's anger was greatly kindled against the man, and he said to Nathan, "As the LORD lives, the man who has done this deserves to die, and he shall restore the lamb fourfold, because he did this thing, and because he had no pity."[xiii]

Nathan then said to David "You are the man!" referring to David having Uriah the Hittite killed in battle in order to cover the sin of David's adultery with Bathsheba.[xiv]

b. Turning peoples' hearts to the LORD.
An angel appeared to Zechariah and told him that Elizabeth, his wife who was barren and advanced in years, would have a child, "[a]nd he [John the Baptist] will turn many of the children of Israel to the Lord their God."[xv]

c. Bringing people back into a covenant relationship with God.
And they abandoned the house of the LORD, the God of their fathers, and served the Asherim and the idols. And wrath came upon Judah and Jerusalem for this guilt of theirs. Yet he sent prophets among them to bring them back to the LORD. These testified against them, but they would not pay attention.[xvi]

d. Warning of what will occur in the future.
Now in these days prophets came down from Jerusalem to Antioch. And one of them named Agabus stood up and foretold by the Spirit that there would be a great famine over all the world (this took place in the days of Claudius). So the disciples determined, every one according to his ability, to send relief to the brothers living in Judea. And they did so, sending it to the elders by the hand of Barnabas and Saul.[xvii]

e. Exhorting and strengthening the brethren.

And Judas and Silas, who were themselves prophets, encouraged and strengthened the brothers with many words.[xviii]

f. Giving divine direction.

Now there were in the church at Antioch prophets and teachers, Barnabas, Simeon who was called Niger, Lucius of Cyrene, Manaen a lifelong friend of Herod the tetrarch, and Saul. While they were worshiping the Lord and fasting, the Holy Spirit said, "Set apart for me Barnabas and Saul for the work to which I have called them." Then after fasting and praying they laid their hands on them and sent them off.[xix]

g. Speaking against sin; warning of judgment, and preaching about hope and renewal.

Then the LORD put out his hand and touched my mouth. And the LORD said to me,
>"Behold, I have put my words in your mouth.
>See, I have set you this day over nations and over kingdoms,
>to pluck up and to break down,
>to destroy and to overthrow,
>to build and to plant."[xx]

Jeremiah's message is threefold: (1) he must **pluck up** and **break down**, which refers to preaching against sin; (2) he must **destroy** and **overthrow**, which relates to messages concerning judgment; and (3) he must **build** and **plant**, which means he must preach about hope and renewal."[xxi]

All prophets do not have the same anointing or spiritual assignments. Some are called to prophesy to the people, some to persons in government, some to individuals, and some to geographic regions, mountains, land, rivers, etc. In addition, some receive prophecies more frequently than others. "Do not despise prophecies, but test everything; hold fast what is good."[xxii]

We are not to blindly accept what is prophesied. In church, "[l]et two or three prophets speak, and let the others weigh what is said. If a revelation is made to another sitting there, let the first be silent. For you can all prophesy one by one, so that all may learn and all be encouraged, and the spirits of prophets are subject to prophets."[xxiii] A prophet may be male or female.[xxiv]

My personal prayer is that you will be enlightened, strengthened, and encouraged as you study this workbook and record what God, Jesus, and The Holy Spirit reveal to you. Time spent with Them along with reading and studying the Bible yields great dividends.

Please check out my new website: **www.sheilaeismann.com**

Also, if you would like to send an email or have questions about this workbook, my address is **sheila@sheilaeismann.com**. Thank you!

"The LORD bless you and keep you;
 The LORD make His face shine upon you,
 And be gracious to you;
 The LORD lift up His countenance upon you,
 And give you peace." (Numbers 6:24-26)

New Year's Dream: The Maze & The Kiss

January 4, 2021
Prophetic Dreams

The eclectic mixture dished up in our dreams can be likened to a smorgasbord if we enjoy those sorts of things. The rural area in which I was raised held an annual one to help raise funds for the local school. Speaking of enjoyment, some people delight in working their way through obstacles, whether on paper or actual courses complete with mud slides, rock climbs, etc. I prayed and asked the Lord to give me a New Year's dream to launch in 2021.

He did in fact give me one before sunrise on January 1st which included the maze and the kiss. How do we marry these up and prepare for the year ahead?

Scene #1:

I needed some salad dressing, so my husband and I decided to go to our local grocery store to get some. It was as if my parents were still alive and in their late 60s to early '70s. We were planning on taking them with us.

For some reason which was not apparent in the dream, just my husband and I drove to the store. Upon entering, and much to my surprise and dismay, there were few items inside. Keep in mind that in real life, this is a major grocery store chain in several states. Normally, the regular shelves and storage areas are piled to the rafters with goods. So for those who like to prepare ahead of time, this would come as a real shock.

What items remained in the store were grouped into categories such as cereal, some canned goods, etc. There were no refrigeration units for perishable items. The merchandise was in the cardboard boxes in which it

was shipped, and those boxes were stacked to form a maze. The side of each box facing the narrow walkway was removed to provide access to the box's contents.

When you walked through the maze, you could just turn to the left or the right and select what you wanted. There were tall, steel reinforcements behind this cardboard structured maze, so there was no way you could high-hurdle or bolt over the sides if one were to get too far into the maze. In addition, the tight passageway was not designed for shopping carts. You could use only a small, plastic basket.

Within seconds of starting into the maze, I looked and did not see any salad dressing. I quickly turned around and exited the store. We never did purchase any groceries.

Scene #2:

As we approached our car in the parking lot, I was startled when I looked about 30 feet to my right and saw my parents and my nephew, Casey, who'd just arrived. They were in his silver, compact pickup.

Casey had parked along the curb of the sidewalk leading into the store. My dad emerged from the pickup wearing his navy-blue jumpsuit which was his signature clothing in the later years of his life. My mother followed closely behind.

I started to walk toward my parents to warn them as to how the store had changed and to give them a "heads up" before their entry. In real life, my dad loved to shop for food as it was the center of so many of our family celebrations and gatherings. Having served in the military, "prepare" was sort of his middle name, along with groceries.

Scene #3:

Casey walked toward me, gave me a big side hug, and a kiss on my left cheek. He said, "I want to invite you to our church service tonight. It's the last one of our special, revival meetings."

End of dream.

FOOD FOR THOUGHT AS WE WORK ON DECIPHERING THIS DREAM:

#1. With the grocery store representing ministry, church, spiritual food supplier, materialistic church, commercial church, or business, I never would have gone into it unless I wanted the salad dressing. Granted, I didn't necessarily need it, but I wanted it. The interesting thing is that I rarely purchase any store-bought dressing as I make my own using ½ cup white balsamic vinegar and ½ cup olive oil. It's absolutely delicious! You should try it. I think you'd like it. If you want to be extra creative, you could take a gander at these instructions for making your own dressing.

https://www.thekitchn.com/how-to-make-a-basic-vinaigrette-226699

Preparation alert: if I wouldn't have entered the store, I would not have known they'd shifted to their sudden, current practices. Like so many other customers these days, I've primarily implemented the "click and pick" procedure wherein you place your order online, drive to the store's parking lot to pick it up, and head back home.

One possible interpretation of salad/salad dressing is negative as it predicts conflicting relations between disease and environment. Bear in mind that diseases can be "manufactured," just like salads and salad dressing.

It does seem a titch odd that I would drive to the store just for salad dressing since it's not something I normally buy. But, then again, I didn't dream up the dream!

This could boil down to one, the all-important word which is conflict.

Sometimes, mazes are not easily navigated. The representation is obvious: feeling lost because there might not be a straightforward way out; trying to find the heart of God in a matter, and a need to walk closely with God to make it safely and successfully through the maze.

The maze also limited or controlled where shoppers could go.

#2. My parents, both of whom accepted Jesus as their personal Lord and Savior before they died, represent the cloud of witnesses who've gone ahead of us. The cloud of witnesses is comprised of those who continue to cheer us in our race of faith to complete our earthly kingdom assignments and fulfill what's written in our books of destiny. (Daniel 7:10; Psalm 139:16; 1 Corinthians 3:11-15; and Ephesians 1:11, 2:10; 4:1.)

Hebrews 12:1-2 instructs, "Therefore we also, since we are surrounded by so great a cloud of witnesses, let us lay aside every weight, and the sin which so easily ensnares *us*, and let us run with endurance the race that is set before us, looking unto Jesus, the author and finisher of *our* faith, who for the joy that was set before Him endured the cross, despising the shame, and has sat down at the right hand of the throne of God."

In real life, I took my parents grocery shopping at three-week intervals for over a decade wherein we actually shopped at one of the chain stores featured in the dream.

Even though my parents are in heaven now, the ages they were in the dream points to how things used to be. This dream is telegraphing that normal procedures will change dramatically in the future.

#3. In real life, Casey is a Christian. He is natural caretaker type of person who exercised his gifting when living near my parents for a decade after he graduated from college. In the dream, he was driving the exact same type of pickup that he purchased upon his college graduation.

I deem one of the main decoding factors of this dream lies in the meaning of Casey's name and accompanying lifetime scripture verse:

"Literal meaning: Brave, watchful.

Suggested Character Quality: Brave, protector. (He was a protector for his maternal grandparents).

Suggested Lifetime Scripture Verse: 1 Thessalonians 5:6, "Therefore let us not sleep, *as others do*, but let us watch and be sober."
The Greek word for sober in this verse is nepho (Strong's G3525) which means to be sober, to be calm and collected in spirit; temperate, dispassionate, circumspect.

https://www.blueletterbible.org/lang/Lexicon/Lexicon.cfm?strongs=G3525&t=KJV

Casey was driving a silver pickup. Automobiles symbolize life, person, or ministry. Silver represents redemption or redemption money. Silver or redemption is the foundation of the Christian life. Silver is not recorded as being in heaven since we need no redemption once we get there.

At the conclusion of the dream, Casey invited me to the last night of his church's revival meeting. One of the main purposes for revival is to help the lost find Jesus and give their lives to Him before it's too late.

#4. There are a plethora of symbols for a kiss which are: empty promises, affection or embrace, seduction, agreement, friend, betrayal, departure/farewell, welcome, greeting, deception, enticement, worship, union/joined, encountering God through worship, covenant, or confession of faith in Christ.

Continuing with the theme of revival and revival meetings, the importance of the kiss reinforces the encountering of God through worship as there's usually praise and worship during revival services. When a confession of faith is made by a new believer, this constitutes a covenant between him or her and God. Many people make this salvation decision during a revival meeting when they're introduced to the true Jesus of the Bible at that time.

The kiss was on my cheek which is symbolic of physical abuse, criticism/blame, testing, suffering when smitten, preparing for persecution, and responding to the same with love.

Prophetic Insights for Daily Living:

When I started my blogs posts, my subtitle became, "Prophetic Insights for Daily Living." To the extent possible in each of them, I try to include some. I hope this has been helpful to you.

A. Remain watchful, circumspect, calm, and collected. (Greek meaning of the word sober.)

B. Who is the Lord stirring your heart and spirit regarding helping watch and protect during 2021?

C. Pray as often and as much as you can. Record answers to your prayers as this is a real faith builder.

D. Continue to read the Holy Bible which is the inerrant word of God. Our spiritual food is just as important as our physical nourishment if not more so. Some religious organizations have their own versions of the Bible, so it's extremely important to read the real Bible and not some distorted version thereof. A great way to prepare for 2021 and beyond is to purchase a Bible if you don't already have one. Our local church freely gives them away each week. Is there anyone the Lord is laying upon your heart to gift a Bible to so they can learn the word of God?

E. Get connected and/or stay with a Bible-believing, Bible-teaching church that does not stray from what the Bible actually teaches and where the leaders will preach without compromising.

F. Pray that churches that have been unable to open can do so and that revival services will become a priority. Millions of people are in the Valley of Decision today (Joel 3:14).

G. A timely book to read in the Bible would be Nehemiah in the Old Testament, so you can find your "place on the wall" and know where and how to serve in the kingdom of God. As you read this book, where you do sense the Lord is asking you to serve?

_____
_____
_____

H. If you discern that you are harboring offenses in your life and are continuing to hold onto resentment, bitterness, and hatred, pray and ask God to break those off you through the power of The Holy Spirit. Offenses are surely to come, and they are like having your hands cuffed and legs in iron shackles. (Luke 17:1-4)

I. Do you have some sort of maze in your life wherein you're trying to find a way out? If so, what is it, and have you discerned how to conquer it? Rest assured, there's never been an earthly maze constructed by oneself or anyone else where there's never been a way for escape. 1 Corinthians 10:13

guarantees us, "No temptation has overtaken you except such as is common to man; but God *is* faithful, who will not allow you to be tempted beyond what you are able, but with the temptation will also make the way of escape, that you may be able to bear *it*."

_____
_____
_____
_____

J. How does this dream speak to you? Can you relate to any aspect of it? Regarding ways to prepare in the natural, yes, that's just common sense. However, the most important type is spiritual readiness.

_____
_____
_____
_____

K. Wisdom is the order of the hour. The only fear we're to have is the holy, reverential fear of God.

https://sheilaeismann.com/dream-therapy/

The book of Proverbs has much to say about wisdom. I consider Wisdom one of my "spiritual mothers or sisters." I want to spend time studying this vital subject. As the mazes of life increase, we can take wisdom by the hand for continued guidance.

Particular Prayer Points for this week January 4-9, 2021 in light of the convergence of 3 main events:

Prayer walks and marches in our nation's capital are scheduled for January 5th and 6th.

Georgia Senate runoff election to be conducted on January 5th.

Congress is scheduled to certify the national election on January 6th.

So, there you have it for the New Year's dream of the maze and the kiss. I tried not to take you through a maze as I was writing it!

If necessary, Jesus can guide us through any maze. We can always trust Him.

Sheila Eismann, Prophetic Seer, Blogger, Author & Teacher, publishes her weekly blog posts endeavoring to encourage others through God's word. Her writings include teaching and instructions on how to apply prophetic insights for daily living. You can subscribe to receive new blog posts on her website at www.sheilaeismann.com.

The Open Gate

January 13, 2021
Prophetic Words

Since I was raised in an agricultural area with cattle, horses, orchards, and fields, sometimes the spiritual messages I receive pertain to that sphere. During my younger days spent on Sage Creek Farms, I wasn't concerned about gaining a heart of wisdom. When reading my devotions on the morning of January 9, 2021, the open gate manifested in front of me. Initially, it was not opened very wide. Every detail of a prophetic vision, dream, or word can have significance.

Early on the 9th, I began silently reading the first few verses of Proverbs 9 which speaks of the Way of Wisdom.

"Wisdom has built her house,
She has hewn out her seven pillars;
She has slaughtered her meat,
She has mixed her wine,
She has also furnished her table.
She has sent out her maidens,
She cries out from the highest places of the city,
'Whoever *is* simple, let him turn in here!'
As for him who lacks understanding, she says to him,
'Come, eat of my bread
And drink of the wine I have mixed.
Forsake foolishness and live,
And go in the way of understanding.'" (Proverbs 9:1-6)

Immediately after reading the word **understanding** which connected with my "internal spiritual tuning fork," the spirit realm opened up, and I saw an old, metal gate that had been painted green at one time. The paint had worn off in some spots which gave it a mottled effect.

The vision took place in a rural, farming area with pastures and fields. The open gate was at the top of an incline. This green gate featured in my blog post isn't open, but it was the closest image I could locate to portray the message.

In the next scene of the vision, a sign was hung on the gate bearing the word

UNDERSTANDING

Scene 3 featured the gate beginning to supernaturally open wider which led to a dirt road behind it. If one were to continue to walk on this, it would take you over the incline into a new vista. The grass was growing on both sides of this road and in the middle where tire tracks did not touch the grass.

End of vision.

I immediately knew by revelation from The Holy Spirit that seeking understanding would open the gate to where you could continue to walk or drive down the road.

The Hebrew word for wisdom is *chokmowth* (Strong's H2454) and is related to the Hebrew word *chokmah* (Strong's H2451) which means:

A. Skill (in war)

B. Wisdom in administration

C. Shrewdness, wisdom

D. Wisdom, prudence (in religious affairs)

E. Wisdom (ethical and religious)

https://www.blueletterbible.org/lang/lexicon/lexicon.cfm?Strongs=H2451

Biynah is one of the Hebrew words (Strong's H998) for understanding which is used in Proverbs 9:6 and means understanding, wisdom, knowledge, perfectly, understand.

https://www.blueletterbible.org/lang/Lexicon/Lexicon.cfm?strongs=H998&t=KJV

As I've contemplated the meanings of wisdom and understanding, what came to me is that while it's great to have wisdom, one still needs to be able to understand what to do with it.

https://sheilaeismann.com/prepare/

From the first six verses of the 9th chapter of Proverbs, there's a clarion call for the simple who lack understanding and have not developed a heart of wisdom to come into her house and take a seat at her table which she has already prepared.

Also, there's an emphasis on going in the way of understanding which indicates there is a definite path or route. It's not just a random one.

In addition, there's a stark contrast between the foolish path and the way of understanding. As with so many other things in life, there's always a critical choice that lies before us every day. And, more importantly, every choice has a consequence. I guess we could call this "The Law of C and C."

Another important consideration is there's God's understanding, and then there's man's understanding. The difference lies in the source. Man's understanding is conjured up in his own mind and controlled by the same.

One of the most referenced verses in the Bible regarding understanding can be found in Proverbs 3:5-6,

"Trust in the LORD with all your heart,
And lean not on your own understanding;
In all your ways acknowledge Him,
And He shall direct your paths."

The prophet Jeremiah aptly describes the human heart,
"The heart *is* deceitful above all *things*,
And desperately wicked;
Who can know it?" (Jeremiah 17:9)

We dare not lean on our own understanding because we're not omniscient and don't have all wisdom. Our lives were never intended to be lived outside of God's guidance, ways, and assistance. They're intentionally purposed to be lived in submission to and reliance upon Him. We're not created to be spiritually all-knowing or all-powerful.

There's a supernatural grace and wisdom which rests upon God's understanding. It comes by revelation through the power of The Holy Spirit as we seek God through His word and prayer with Him. He's just waiting for us to call or check in with Him each day. (Jeremiah 33:3) His line is never busy and there's no voice mail box in heaven! It's by God's design that we are given a limited understanding of most things. Otherwise, we may adopt the attitude, "Thanks, God, I've got this and can take it from here."

Were you in a red, hot hurry to shed the year 2020 and turn the calendar to this month? Every new year holds so much hope and promise, yet it needs to be navigated with supreme understanding to accomplish the overarching goal of attaining a heart of wisdom.

_____
_____
_____
_____

Financial planners, medical advisors, educators, and many others advise folks to "take stock or plan" for the year ahead.

I think it's important to ask ourselves if we lack understanding or need wisdom in any area of our lives at the moment. To that end, pretend that I'm talking with you on the phone. If I asked you to fill in the spaces below, what would you say or write in answer to my questions:

"What (gate of) understanding do you need to be opened right now?"

_____
_____
_____
_____
_____

"Is there a path or road of understanding that you need to follow or pursue in 2021? If so, what would it be, and what's your plan moving forward?"

_____
_____
_____
_____
_____

In the prophetic vision, the gate is connected to a road or path of understanding. There's no way to know what is beyond the gate until we start down the road. The prophet Jeremiah had some sage advice in the 16th verse of the 6th chapter,

"Thus says the LORD:

'Stand in the ways and see,
And ask for the old paths, where the good way *is*,

And walk in it;
Then you will find rest for your souls.
But they (Israel) said, 'We will not walk *in it.*'"

As strange as it may sound, every solution to any problem in life can be found in the pages of the Bible from the books of Genesis to Revelation. The inerrant word of God contains His understanding which transcends time, culture, civilizations, geography, or anything else.

The Holy Spirit helps us to understand the Bible as we read and study it. Personal and corporate prophecies can lend wisdom, guidance, and insight. It's important to keep in mind that these will never contradict God's word.

When we accept Jesus Christ of Nazareth as our personal Lord and Savior, we are indwelt with The Holy Spirit Who becomes our teacher. (John 14:16; 1 John 2:27; Ephesians 1:13-14.)

For me personally, I've discovered a very interesting aspect to understanding. Even if I can't change something, if I can understand the "why" of it, this helps me in an emotional sense.

Gates can symbolize a plethora of things such as authority, power, opportunity, access, etc. In fact, when I consulted the prophetic resources in my library while writing this week's blog post, I discovered there are over 40 of them!

The book of Nehemiah speaks of the fish gate, sheep gate, horse gate, water gate, and many others. Each of these had a specific use. It's interesting to me how many times the word **_gate_** is used in the Old Testament. I would say gates are quite important to God.

Proverbs is chock full of common sense, wisdom, understanding, and direction. A little over thirty years ago, my husband and I attended a weekly Bible Study hosted by our spiritual parents, Jim and Ruby. The meetings were typically held in their home; however, one evening it was hosted by their nearby neighbors, Lee and Margene.

In attendance that night was a pastor's wife named Beverly. She was the mother of five daughters. During the time of our study, she made a suggestion which I still implement: read the chapter of the book of Proverbs corresponding to the day of the month of the current calendar.

Prophetic Insights for Daily Living:

On the subject of Proverbs, verse 9:3b states that wisdom cries out from the highest places of the city. There were so many voices during 2020 that it shredded and clouded the atmosphere in most areas. The beautiful aspect of shutting out the noise and quieting ourselves before the Lord is that we can hear what He is saying to us by and through The Holy Spirit Who will not compete with the clamor of the world.

My Hebrews 3:13 exhortation would be to set aside some quiet time every day to seek God and read the Bible if you're not already doing so. You'll be amazed at the benefits! "Wisdom rests in the heart of him who has understanding," (Proverbs 14:33a)

Sheila Eismann, Prophetic Seer, Blogger, Author & Teacher, publishes her weekly blog posts endeavoring to encourage others through God's word. Her writings include teaching and instructions on how to apply prophetic insights for daily living. You can subscribe to receive new blog posts on her website at www.sheilaeismann.com.

The Sea, The Bottle, & The Scroll

January 18, 2021
Prophetic Visions

Rarely do I receive visions while driving, but on the 14th of this month, the Spirit realm opened up wherein I received a three-part vision of the sea, the bottle, and the scroll. These were fascinating clues to work on this spiritual puzzle.

In the first scene, I saw where the sea was awash with debris and rubbish which had floated to the top. It was so thick; you couldn't even see the water.

Scene two featured a small bottle shaped like an old-fashioned, transparent soda bottle that had been sealed with red wax. The top was big enough that you could chip the wax off, and fish something from inside.

In the final part of this vision, I could see a thin, beige-colored piece of parchment paper. It was rolled up tightly and secured with a red, waxed seal.

The bottle washed up on the shore just waiting to be discovered.

End of vision.

Fortunately, while driving, I was near a stop light that turned red and stayed that way for close to four minutes, so I could record the vision. Years ago, I'd made a habit of maintaining one of those small notebooks inside the console of the front seat of our car. They come in very handy for occasions such as this one.

As I continued to drive, two scriptures were quickened unto me:

#1. Psalm 103:12, "As far as the east is from the west, *So* far has He removed our transgressions from us."

#2. Acts 3:19, "Repent therefore and be converted, that your sins may be blotted out, so that times of refreshing may come from the presence of the Lord,"

*** Since this was given to me on the 14th day of the month, and with that number symbolizing deliverance and liberty, it speaks of God delivering someone from his sins and/or an ongoing sinful lifestyle.

Upon accepting Jesus Christ of Nazareth as our personal Lord and Savior, our sins are forgiven; all of the old things have passed away, and we become new creations in Him. (2 Corinthians 5:17). We put off the old man, and become a new one. (Ephesians 4:22-24)

God does His part by forgiving us after we come to Jesus, but we must do our part by turning our backs on sin and developing spiritually healthy lifestyles. I'd like to give you an agricultural analogy if I may. Sometimes on our farm, something would get wrapped around the axle of a trailer which meant we had to stop the tractor we were driving and remove whatever was causing the problem before we could continue with our tasks. Do you have any sin wrapped around your life or something impeding your progress?

_____
_____
_____

Another word picture would be a large, heavy, steel ball bearing the word **SIN** which is chained to our ankle. This would definitely affect our daily walk. We need to ask ourselves, "Who and/or what is influencing and controlling my life?"

_____
_____
_____
_____

All of us can be thankful for this reminder, 1 John 2:1-2, "My little children, these things I write to you, so that you may not sin. And if anyone sins, we have an Advocate with the Father, Jesus Christ the righteous. And He Himself is the propitiation for our sins, and not for ours only but also the whole world."

*** The sea is symbolic of the (sea of) humanity, the unbelieving world, and baptism. There's no interpretation needed for the junk that was fully floating across the top of it.

*** **Bottles** reflect the heart. Old bottles indicate the old self, deception, or friendship. James 4:4 warns us that friendship with the world is enmity with God. We're to live in the world but not be of the world. As pilgrims, we're merely passing through this earth en route to heaven. (1 Chronicles 29:15; 1 Peter 2:11-12)

*** Inside the bottle was a beautiful, parchment scroll that represents the word of God, ancient books, and personal calling or destiny. Parchment signals antiquity.

The image of the bottle in this blog post was not sealed with red wax; however, it was the closest one I could find to portray the prophetic message.

As a writer, I enjoy penning and sending personal notes. In the pre-Covid days when it was much easier to gather for luncheons and family events, I loved melting a piece of wax on the back of an envelope containing a greeting card before I affixed my "S" seal. It just looked so fancy!

*** In the vision, the seal on the scroll was red which speaks of redemption (Jesus' blood shed on the cross for our sins).

On the afternoon of the 14th of January, it was quickened unto me the reason for the one-page scroll. It's because it details two things:

A. Our individual, particular assignment(s) for 2021 as we continue to complete our books of destiny.

B. At least one of the nine fruits outlined in Galatians 5:22-23 which the Holy Spirit will be developing in greater measure within us. This will be either be love, joy, peace, longsuffering, kindness, goodness, faithfulness, gentleness, or self-control. Just as with raising fruit in a natural orchard, there's pruning that's required ahead of a growing season. Trust me when I can tell you that it's fairly easy to discern which fruit He's targeting because you can usually feel it within yourself! An obvious example of this would be longsuffering when we find ourselves continually short of patience.

C. The Holy Spirit will give us specific instructions and aid us with how to further develop this fruit which will become evident to all. You will smile inwardly if someone happens to comment, "Wow, you sure seem to be more joyful lately!"

*** The number 21 is like a double-sided coin. As with so many other things in life, there's a negative aspect to it as well as a positive. The negative is exceedingly sinfulness of sin. I surmise this is why the sea was chock full of litter and debris. The positive symbolism is the fullness or completion of spiritual perfection. By perfection, I mean spiritual maturity. Other representations of 21 are expecting God and serving Him.

*** Another positive symbol of fourteen (the date I received this prophetic vision) is a double measure of spiritual perfection (maturity) which is much easier to achieve when we make the conscious decision to put a destructive, sinful lifestyle behind us. The only way we can do this is by and through the power of The Holy Spirit Who indwells us after we become believers in Jesus Christ.

In previous blog posts, I've mentioned the book(s) of destiny each of us has in heaven which were written before the foundation of the world. One of the main considerations for these books is there's an anointed and appointed time to fulfill what's written on the pages within the covers of them. In other words, it's dangerous to adopt the attitude that we'll get around to doing what God has called us to do on our timetable and when we feel like it.

Ultimately, the books of destiny will be closed when we pass away. They won't be opened again until the end of time when every person will be judged accordingly. (Romans 14:10-12; 2 Corinthians 5:9-10; and Revelation 20:11-15)

https://sheilaeismann.com/prepare/

What do you do if you have no clue what's written in your destiny books? As I've pondered this, a very logical thought occurred to me. God would not have issued books to us if they were not intended to be discovered and completed. It would be like a school teacher issuing textbooks at the start of a school year and never passing them out so that students could read and study them. They would just sit on the shelf or inside a backpack and collect dust. There's no profit or fulfillment in that!

The prophet reminds us in Jeremiah 29:11-13, "For I know the thoughts that I think toward you, says the Lord, thoughts of peace and not of evil, to give you a future and a hope. Then you will call upon Me and go and pray to Me, and I will listen to you. And you will seek Me and find *Me,* when you search for Me with all your heart."

I can personally guarantee you this: when you set aside time to seek God with your whole, undivided heart, He will indeed show you what's in your books of destiny. When He fashioned you in your mother's womb (Psalm 139:16), He wrote your books of destiny at the very same time. Some of the information in your books will include your kingdom assignments here on earth.

As you've read, pondered, and studied this blog post and scripture, what is written in your book(s) of destiny?

_____
_____
_____
_____

Matthew 25:14-30 is also instructive and insightful regarding this subject. I would encourage you to spend some time reading these verses and allow The Holy Spirit to bring spiritual revelation to you regarding your talents. Everybody has them, and they are different for all of us.

https://www.biblegateway.com/passage/?search=Matthew%2025%3A14-30&version=NKJV

*** The scroll inside the bottle which washed to the shore is just like our books in heaven. It's been preserved in the bottle until the appointed time of opening which is now, and it is like a treasure hunt that will help us to complete our spiritual puzzle.

Prophetic Insights For Daily Living:

Print off this blog post which will help serve as a reminder of your scroll and books of destiny.

Throughout this year, record your progress and the revelation that you receive from The Holy Spirit.

_____
_____
_____
_____

I'd like to mention two fun aspects of this vision which were also fascinating clues to solve the spiritual puzzle. I was traveling on Horseshoe Road across from a carwash when I received the revelatory download. Since cars represent our lives and horseshoes are formed in the fire, isn't it interesting that just as our cars need to be washed, our lives can be washed daily by reading the word of God (Ephesians 5:26) and purified by the fire of The Holy Spirit (Matthew 3:11)?

_____
_____

A helpful prayer you can pray, but don't do this until you are ready with full intentions in your heart: "Father, I ask you to remove everyone and everything from me that's unholy, unprofitable, and unclean. Restore (from the old) and bring forth from the new that which is holy, profitable, and clean." This verbiage was downloaded to my spirit about a decade ago. It took courage to exercise this prayer with full intentions, but when I did, the results were amazing! It was as if a pair of rose-colored glasses were removed, and I could finally see some things for what they really were.
If you prayed this prayer, please record what answers you received:

My personal invitation: I'd love to hear from you regarding your discoveries of what's in your books of destiny or which fruit is being grown in your life. Please send your email to: sheila@sheilaeismann.com

Sheila Eismann, Prophetic Seer, Blogger, Author & Teacher, publishes her weekly blog posts endeavoring to encourage others through God's word. Her writings include teaching and instructions on how to apply prophetic insights for daily living. You can subscribe to receive new blog posts on her website at www.sheilaeismann.com.

Prophetic Vision: A Blank Bank Check

January 26, 2021
Prophetic Visions

Do you put much stock in a personalized blank, bank check or are you the type that doesn't particularly care? Beyond that, do you even use checks anymore since many people pay for most things electronically these days? For some banking insight, continue reading.

Upon awakening the morning of January 23, 2021, the Spirit realm opened up, and I received the following vision:

A blank check appeared before me in the Spirit revealing these specific things:

A white background
A bold, red border all the way around the check
Bearing the check number 175

Two-thirds of the way down on the left-hand side where the name of the institution is normally listed, the words, **Thomas Edward Bank,** appeared in bold, blue ink on the first line, and **Est. 1876** on the second.

As near as I could determine in real life, there's never been a bank bearing the name of Thomas Edward.

A lot of the time, what manifests in the Spirit realm parallels what's going on in the physical one. Since there's not a bank with the name Thomas Edward, I deem more emphasis should be given to the spiritual aspect.

A brief history of America's banking industry:

Quite possibly, one of the first questions we might want to ask is, "What was significant about the year 1876 as it pertained to the banking industry in our country?"

The ending of the American Civil War on May 9, 1865, gave rise to the railroad construction boom.

35,000 miles of new tracks were laid across the country between approximately the years 1866-1873.

With railroads being the country's largest non-agricultural employers, various industries, including banks, were investing their money into railroads.

The first transcontinental railroad was completed on May 10, 1869. Jay Cooke & Company, a major bank, invested heavily in the construction of a second transcontinental railroad, but it was forced into bankruptcy on September 18, 1873, resulting in a panic in which at least 100 banks failed when depositors demanded their money.

With roughly 25% of the nation's railroads falling into bankruptcy and 18,000 businesses failing in two years, nationwide unemployment had risen to 14% by 1876.

Ulysses S. Grant, the 18th President of our country, served from March 4, 1869, until March 4, 1877. Dark, heavy economic clouds hung over Grant's second term of office. He took sides with the business leaders from the eastern part of our country. Their cumulative ideas did not mitigate the continuing financial disaster.

When Grant departed from office in 1877, the ongoing nationwide financial depression sparked massive railroad strikes which brought the trains to a screeching halt.

Rutherford B. Hayes, who served as our country's 19th president from 1877 to 1881, sent federal troops to several states to stop the railroad strikes. The altercations left many dead and injured.

The American landscape changed dramatically following the Civil War with the advent of the industrial revolution wherein many people moved from the rural areas to cities.

Here were some major factors/considerations for creating the National Bank Act in 1863, thirteen years before the information on the check (1876) which appeared in the Spirit on January 23, 2021:

Provide federal war loans
Establishment of a national currency
Mitigation of the financial crisis during the Civil War
Suspension by banks of payments in gold or silver coins for paper currency (bills or notes) in December of 1861
The inability of Americans to convert bank notes into coins

The Legal Tender Act of 1862 allowed the government to issue paper money (greenbacks) that was not backed by gold or silver and required creditors to accept it at face value.

If you would like further information on the National Banking System, you can read all about it below!

https://www.lancasterschools.org/cms/lib/NY19000266/Centricity/Domain/295/04_NationalBankAct.pdf

The Federal Reserve Act was enacted in 1913 which created the Federal Reserve System. It is still in force and effect today.

Plugging in some symbolism for this prophetic vision:

Banks are symbolic of heaven which is God's treasury; Jesus; sure thing ("You can take it to the bank!"); wealth or money; your place of employment; a storehouse; or your heart.

Regarding the blank bank check, red, white, and blue signal patriotism as those are America's colors. Individually, red speaks of redemption, blue of the color of heaven, and white is purity, holiness, and righteousness.

There's no exact interpretation for the number 175. Putting the three numbers together, we find that 100 symbolizes the children of the promise;

70 represents perfection (maturity) of the spiritual order; release from captivity

(Israel was in captivity in Babylon for 70 years – Jeremiah chapters 20-22; 24-29; 34-35; and 52); an increase; and complete rest. 5 is God's grace to man and man's responsibility, abundance, favor, and multi-tasking.

Portions of the check were incomplete such as the date, the name on the account, the amount of the check, the memo in the lower left-hand corner to indicate why the money was being spent, and the signature.

A blank check could emphasize the verbiage, "You have a blank check to do whatever or to purchase anything you desire." In other words, there's no limit. The account cannot be overdrawn.

Money is one of those symbolisms which has either a real strong, positive aspect or negative one.

Positive:

#1. Faith

#2. Gifts or talents

#3. Blessing as a result of putting God first in your life

#4. Planting a seed and how you use it

#5. Purchase rights

#6. Making a sacrifice or offering

Negative:

#1. Greed which negates a person's spiritual life

#2. Worldly power

#3. Bribes

#4. The love of it which is the root of all evil (1 Timothy 6:10)

#5. Conducting commercial activity in church (Matthew 21:12 where Jesus entered the temple and overturned the tables of the moneychangers)

#6. Can lead to a betrayal depending upon which master one chooses. Jesus warns that we cannot serve two masters, i.e., Him or mammon. We must choose one or the other, however. (Matthew 6:24)

On the basic subject of money, there's nothing inherently wrong with it as it's the Lord our God who gives us the ability to get wealth according to Deuteronomy 8:18. "And you shall remember the Lord your God, for *it is* He who gives you power to get wealth, that He may establish His covenant which He swore to your fathers, as *it is* this day."

Do you deem there's a slight temptation to emphasize just the first part of this verse about the ability to get the wealth from God without consideration of how we can use it to help establish His (New Testament) covenant on the earth today?

_____
_____
_____
_____

The defining aspect of wealth and money is a heart issue as most things in life ultimately boil down to these.

How do you view money in your heart? There's really no way to hide this for any extended period of time because ultimately the fruit of our life will reveal it.

_____
_____
_____
_____

https://sheilaeismann.com/snare-alert/

Decoding the blank bank check prophetic vision:

A major clue to decoding this prophetic vision could reside within the meaning of the name of the bank on the check.

Thomas' name appeared first, and the literal meaning of his name means *A Twin*. The suggested character quality is a seeker of truth and accompanying lifetime scripture verse is Psalm 63:1,

"O God, You *are* my God;
Early will I seek You;
My soul thirsts for You;
My flesh longs for You
In a dry and thirsty land
Where there is no water."

Since my family lives in the desert, I can attest to how valuable water is. Growing up and working long hours in the fields on Sage Creek Farms, there were times when I became very thirsty if I'd forgotten to bring along some water. I couldn't wait to get home and drink from a cool water pitcher, especially during July when harvesting hay for our cows. Some days were literally 101 degrees in the shade with no shade!

Edward portrays a prosperous guardian for both the literal meaning of the name along with the suggested character quality. Psalm 37:37 rounds out the lifetime scripture verse,

"Mark the blameless *man,* and observe the upright;
For the future of *that* man *is* peace."

How important is absolute truth to you? Have you ever believed something so intently only to find out it was completely false? Can you recall how you felt after you found out you'd been duped?

Truth is a choice with very real, daily consequences. Absolute truth can only be found in God's word. There's an additional point regarding this as truth is not man's opinion of God's word. This is how cults are sometimes formed.

The name Thomas means *A Twin* which could be the two sides of truth, i.e., objective truth (God's word) and subjective truth (man's opinion of God's word). Or take any other random topic as the same test can be applied. Have you ever subscribed to subjective truth? If so, what was it, and what did it take to correct it? How long did this process take?

_____
_____
_____
_____

This is a pretty zany example, but it does serve the purpose of my query in this week's blog post. Suppose you subjectively believed that the earth was flat. If you took a trip around the world, even if it wasn't in 80 days, you would come to your point of destination. If the world was flat, you'd fall off the edge into space!

https://pioneersofflight.si.edu/content/first-flight-around-world-0

Truth is the first emphasis in the name of the bank on the blank check. The second one is observing the life of a righteous man which leads to peace even amid chaos and calamity. Psalm 37, which accompanies the name Edward, is chock full of truth and Godly wisdom. There's a stark contrast in the verses regarding a righteous man versus a wicked one.

Our spiritual bank accounts compared to our physical ones:

I love reading the first chapter of the book of Ephesians as it makes me feel like one of the world's wealthiest people! In my account, I have redemption, forgiveness, grace, wisdom, prudence, inheritance, and adoption into the kingdom of heaven where I have a permanent seat at the table.

We have a choice as to where we bank while here on earth, both physically and spiritually. A physical choice would be XYZ bank, for example, and after accepting Jesus Christ as our personal Lord and Savior, we open our spiritual bank account which already has our deposits frontloaded. Wow, talk about a good deal!

Unlike our physical banks which may have limited funds in them from time to time, our heavenly bank accounts are limitless and cannot be overdrawn.

Prophetic Insights for Daily Living:

Every bank has a brand and reputation. Typically, there's a slogan that accompanies the bank's name.

Inherent within the message from the Lord via this prophetic vision is an invitation that reads,

"You are invited to open an account with **_Thomas Edward Bank_** where you're guaranteed God's truth and a prosperous spiritual future."

This timely prophetic vision is challenging all of us to examine where we're "spiritually banking" as our true treasures are to be stored in heaven. (Matthew 6:21)

How has this prophetic vision and message challenged you?

_____
_____
_____
_____

Sheila Eismann, Prophetic Seer, Blogger, Author & Teacher, publishes her weekly blog posts endeavoring to encourage others through God's word. Her writings include teaching and instructions on how to apply prophetic insights for daily living. You can subscribe to receive new blog posts on her website at www.sheilaeismann.com.

Prophetic Vision: Hot-Off-The-Press

February 2, 2021
Prophetic Visions

Do you happen to recall the riddle from decades ago, "What's black and white, and read all over?" If one were to just hear this question and not read it, you might think that it pertained to the color red as opposed to the verb read. No wonder the English language is so hard to learn!

I was given a prophetic vision recently which bore the hot-off-the-press newspaper headlines, "Forsake Foolishness And Live!" This was after I'd been hearing the phrase off and on for about the past month.

Scene #1:

In this prophetic vision, countless newspapers were rolling off a large press. It was sort of like those old movie reels from the 1940s and 1950s showing major announcements during a time frame in which people read more daily papers than they do now.

The verbiage, "Forsake foolishness and live" comes from Proverbs 9:1-6.

"Wisdom has built her house,
She has hewn out her seven pillars;
She has slaughtered her meat,
She has mixed her wine,
She has also furnished her table.
She has sent out her maidens,
She cries out from the highest places of the city,

'Whoever *is* simple, let him turn in here!'
As for him who lacks understanding, she says to him,
'Come, eat of my bread
And drink of the wine I have mixed.
Forsake foolishness and live,
And go in the way of understanding.'"

Proverbs Chapter 9 makes a stark contrast between the way of wisdom and the way of folly. There are other means this could be interpreted such as the narrow path of life and the broad path of destruction (Matthew 7:13-14).

Has mankind always needed wisdom? Well, of course! It's readily apparent from this vision that the clarion call is louder now than ever before. In reading the above verses, it's as if wisdom has a voice that we can hear. This is why it's so important for all of us to evaluate who and/or what we are listening to daily.

The symbolisms for a newspaper are God's word, headlines, public exposure, gossip, or listening to the world. The urgent invitation is to shut out the white noise from the world, press in, and hear wisdom's voice. She has a heavenly frequency all her own. Have you heard it?

_____

_____

_____

In my case, for the past 2-3 months I'd posed a question to the Lord requiring much wisdom. As I was waiting on Him for a response, I began to repeatedly hear "Forsake foolishness and live." I guess you could say I received His definitive response. There was no guesswork involved after that.

Pray and ask God to help you hear wisdom's voice. There are many ways that He speaks whether through dreams, visions, a distinct impression made upon our mind or spirit, or supernaturally deposited within our heart (Nehemiah 7:5) or spirit, a prophetic word spoken through a fellow believer, a passage of scripture, songs, or a prophetic sign such as Jonah on the ship before he was swallowed by the whale. (Jonah 1:1-17)

In addition, you can hear an audible voice according to Isaiah 30:21,

"Your ears shall hear a word behind you, saying,
'This *is* the way, walk in it,'
Whenever you turn to the right hand
Or whenever you turn to the left."

Companion verses to Isaiah 30:21 are Psalm 143:8 and Proverbs 2:6.

The Holy Spirit gives gifts of words of knowledge and wisdom when needed. (1 Corinthians 12:8) It's fine and dandy to have knowledge, but wisdom to know what to do with it is paramount as well. Matthew 7:7-11 guarantees that God will answer when we seek Him.

<u>Scene #2:</u>

In the next scene of the vision, I saw four footsteps in the snow walking forward and 11 walking backward. Since they appeared in the snow, I deem this is a "Now Word" since we're in winter.

https://sheilaeismann.com/seek-the-lost/

Four is symbolic of worldwide, creation, universal, and an open door. These steps would appear to be walking forward in wisdom and understanding.

Eleven represents judgment, disorder, disintegration, and incompleteness which would signal walking backward due to lack of wisdom and choosing foolishness.

Have you ever experienced a time in your life when you made a decision that seemed to gain forward momentum only to discover it was an unwise choice, so you went twice as far backward and lost ground? If so, when was it, and what did you learn from it?

_____
_____
_____
_____

There's an inherent warning within these verses from Proverbs that if we want to live, we must forsake foolishness. Yes, we can live without wisdom, but can we really live our lives to the fullest extent and fulfill our God-given destiny? Foolishness can also lead to eternal death as opposed to eternal life in heaven with Jesus our Lord and Savior.

Within the scripture passage, it's almost like wisdom is asking us to make a vow with her, not unlike a marriage vow which goes something along the lines of, "forsaking all others and pledging myself to you for as long as we both shall live." In a sense, would you rather be married to wisdom or foolishness?

_____

_____

_____

The Bible has SO much to say about the subject of wisdom that it's definitely a challenge to keep it short within a weekly blog post. Since the newspaper headlines read the way they did, one can infer that something must be done after the forsaking. The instruction appears in the next line which is to go in the way of understanding. A person can have understanding and knowledge, but without wisdom, sometimes we don't know how to apply it or what to do with it.

https://sheilaeismann.com/heart-of-wisdom/

Why do you think that the vision manifested as words in a newspaper headline as opposed to on the internet or mobile phone or audibly heard on the radio?

The importance of discerning the different types of wisdom:

Thankfully, the apostle James instructs us regarding this all-important matter in James 3:13-18. Basically, there are two categories. We can tell the difference by the fruit which is produced.

#1. Demonic or earthly wisdom yields bitter envy, self-seeking, boasting, lying, confusion, and every evil thing. The words "every evil thing" would entail quite a bit. Ponder that for a short while.

#2. Heavenly wisdom is pure, peaceable, gentle, willing to yield, full of mercy and good fruits, without partiality and without hypocrisy, and yields works done in meekness (Godly strength). Godly wisdom is not how to gain the things of the world as we're to be storing up treasures in heaven. (Matthew 6:19-21)

As the ol' saying goes, "You don't have to be a rocket scientist to figure that one out!"

Prophetic insights for daily living:

Assess your life today. In which area do you need wisdom?
_____

Pray and ask God for spiritual and practical help.

Record and act upon exactly what He shows you to do listing all of the specifics, so you can refer to it later if necessary.

_____

_____

_____

_____

He will be faithful to send you confirmation of His leading and instructions.

Be on the lookout for them as they sometimes surface when and where we least expect them.

Go back later, and review this to see how He answers and delivers.

Purpose in your heart to do a topical Bible study on the subject. For example, if you need wisdom regarding finances, drill down on what the word of God has to say. With respect to money matters, The Bible has more than 2,350 verses dealing with money, property, and related matters.

https://irp-cdn.multiscreensite.com/c21a6153/files/uploaded/250BibleVersesAboutMoney.pdf

Walking in and exercising wisdom is like daily exercise. It's not a one-and-done sort of thing. It needs to become a healthy, lifetime habit.

If we've been foolish in any area of our lives, it's never too late to change course and go in the way of understanding. Inherent within wisdom are healing, forgiveness, restoration, redemption, and mercy.

Faith without good works is dead (James 2:14-17). Are you willing to lend a helping hand to someone who needs to forsake foolishness and find wisdom? If you've had a life experience where you've been foolish but later gained wisdom, are you willing to mentor or introduce someone to wisdom's ways? Blessings will run both ways through the channel on that one.

_____

_____

_____

Jesus said that wisdom is justified by all her children. (Luke 7:35) Ergo, I want wisdom to be one of my spiritual mothers. I hope you do, too!

Sheila Eismann, Prophetic Seer, Blogger, Author & Teacher, publishes her weekly blog posts endeavoring to encourage others through God's word. Her writings include teaching and instructions on how to apply prophetic insights for daily living. You can subscribe to receive new blog posts on her website at www.sheilaeismann.com.

Sheila Eismann

During February: Tweak Your Wheelhouses

February 8, 2021
Prophetic Words

There are at least three repetitive themes that seem to be emerging in Christendom as of late which are pioneering, standing firm, and wisdom. As I've continued to wait on the Lord regarding both of these and pray into them, the following was impressed upon my spirit by The Holy Spirit, "Tweak Your Wheelhouses." It's time to evaluate, el pronto!

The verbiage *tweak* seems to be one of modern-day- vernacular whereas *wheelhouse* stems from decades ago. What's a wheelhouse anyway?

1. A part of a boat or ship serving as a shelter for the person at the wheel.

2. One's area of interest or expertise.

https://www.google.com/search?q=what+is+a+wheelhouse&oq=what+is+a+wheelhouse&aqs=chrome..69i57j0l4j0i22i30l5.2477j1j7&sourceid=chrome&ie=UTF-8

Unless you're in the military or a shipmaster, and for the purposes of this week's blog post, I'll be referencing the second definition listed above.

While we're on the subject of word meanings, what's listed for the verb aspect of tweak?

1. Twist or pull (something) sharply. "He tweaked the boy's ear."

2. Informal (usage): To improve (a mechanism or system) by making fine adjustments to it. "Engineers tweak the car's operating systems during the race."

https://www.google.com/search?q=definition+of+tweak&rlz=1C1CHBF_enUS800US801&oq=definition+of+tweak&aqs=chrome..69i57j0l3j0i22i30l6.2927j1j9&sourceid=chrome&ie=UTF-8

What's interesting regarding the prophetic word I heard was the term "tweak." Again, regarding the definitions listed above, my emphasis is upon the second one which is improving or fine-tuning.

Since the physical or natural realms mirror the spiritual one, we can have spiritual wheelhouses or areas of interest and expertise.

With the current monthly directive given, it's important to evaluate each of them as it applies to our lives.

To improve or fine-tune something, one must have a general sense and working knowledge of it in the first place. In other words, how could I tweak a wheelhouse in road construction or designing guitars if I had no experience or frame of reference of these to begin with?

The necessity for tweaking our wheelhouses is not just as a result of the worldwide pandemic, but the drastically changing landscape on several fronts. Perhaps this is why there's a concert of voices singing the same tunes recently which are:

"Stand firm, and don't be shaken like a reed in the wind."

https://sheilaeismann.com/unshakeable/

"Revisit the pioneer days of the past."

"Though it cost all you have, get wisdom."

For the sake of discussion and to evaluate, let's just choose a fictional character named Lizbea. Her physical wheelhouse is an interior decorator and the gift of helps or serving is her spiritual one. (1 Corinthians 12:28; Romans 12:7)

Many folks have flown the coop, so to speak, in Lizbea's geographic region due to high taxes and pandemic fallout. The demand for her services has all but dwindled. In addition, the state in which she resides has beyond strict pandemic restrictions. She doesn't want to put her Interior Design college degree on the shelf, so she must don her thinking cap.

If you were advising Lizbea as to how she could still stay afloat financially and improve or make fine adjustments to her business, what would you tell her?

_____
_____

One possibility would be for her to design an online course and proceed accordingly. Granted, she'd have to do some background work and research to get this launched, but it would be a major "tweak," so to speak. I'm just waxing a little poetic on that one!

Navigating the pandemic, Lizbea could contact some of the existing business owners in her locale who've not exited and ask for the opportunity to design some window displays, online or in-store ones.

A third suggestion might be for Lizbea to reconnect with some of her college buddies through a zoom call for a brainstorming session since they might all be in the same boat. Maybe not the same wheelhouse, but the same boat, figuratively speaking.

While the above suggestions might be ultra-elementary, you get the idea.

Having read this far through my blog post, you might be saying to yourself, "Well, I know what my physical wheelhouse is, but I have no clue what my spiritual one could be."

I have fantastic news for you! That's where God, Jesus, The Holy Spirit, and The Bible enter the situation. God designed each of us with unique gifts, talents, abilities, and desires. No two of us on the planet are 100% alike.

Back to Lizbea for a moment. Her spiritual gift is primarily that of helps or serving. These types of gifts are also known as "The Motivational Gifts" as they are what motivates each one of us. Romans 12:6-8 lists the gifts, and 1 Peter 4:10 is a companion verse.

You can examine your own life and probably readily discern what your giftings are just by observing or listing what you do on a regular basis or the types of things you instinctively respond to. Someone with the gift of helps or services renders practical service in almost every situation. It's usually their first response in any given circumstance, especially a crisis.

On a personal note, a family member recently passed. Our friends and family members who have the motivational/spiritual gift of helps contacted us right away to offer their assistance of whatever was needed.

A great resource that I highly recommend if you'd like further information regarding your giftings is the book titled *Discover Your God-Given Gifts* by Don and Katie Fortune. My husband and I have both used this book in prior Bible Study classes which we've taught over the years.

https://www.amazon.com/Discover-Your-God-Given-Gifts-Fortune/dp/0800794672/ref=sr_1_1?crid=27D62S92DJTFK&dchild=1&keywords=discover+your+god+given+gifts+fortune&qid=1612642298&sprefix=discover+your+god+%2Caps%2C234&sr=8-1

Exercising our physical and spiritual giftings makes us feel much better as a person as we are contributing to mankind and the kingdom of God simultaneously along with fulfilling our God-given destiny.

After the passing of our family member, one of our dear Christian sisters rang the doorbell one day. I just happened to be passing from our office into the living room and saw her from inside our entryway window. She'd baked a yummy apple strudel loaf and decorated it with aluminum foil tied with red yarn, so it looked like a cross!

This particular sister knows how I love birds, so she'd carefully hand-selected a beautiful card and penned such caring, comforting words. These items were lovingly placed inside a box lined with tissue paper and left on the table on our front steps. With Meredith's gift of serving and helps, she'd put a lot of tender, loving care into her "special delivery." I just sat down and cried as I thought of Jesus expressing His care and comfort for us through a friend exercising her gifting.

Continuing with Lizbea, she's really sort of in a bind now, isn't she? Servers and helpers are used to being on the go as they render practical help. Amid the pandemic, how can Lizbea fine-tune this gifting? One of the easiest things for her to do is when the situation arises, pray and ask God what He would have her to do. He's the One Who sees the whole big picture. God may direct her to prepare some meals which could be easily frozen, so when the pandemic wanes, she can be "at the ready" to help families in need.

The word of the Lord does not come forth unless it's important and instructional. Obviously, we're going to need to tweak our wheelhouses to navigate the days ahead. The landscape is changing like quicksand under our feet with each passing day. Perhaps you're way ahead of the curve and have been doing this already to which I say, "Hallelujah, keep tweaking!"

One of the many things I love about God is that He does not ask us to do something if He doesn't already have the answers in His pipeline. (Isaiah 65:24) Since He uniquely fashioned each one of us (Psalm 139:16), His answers are going to be different. It's not a *one size fits all* deal.

Godly wisdom is supreme and should be implemented ahead of man's wisdom. If He's instructing us regarding our wheelhouses which He gave us in the first place, it's important that we consult Him. In last week's blog post, I wrote about the difference between heavenly and earthly wisdom. The proof is in the fruit.

To keep our wheelhouses humming along smoothly, fresh winds and words from the throne room of God are released in a timely fashion. What are the inherent benefits for us?

a. Lessens frustration.

b. Retains balance in our bodies, souls, minds, and spirits.

c. Maintains hope and joy.

d. Renders assistance to fulfill our books of destiny.

e. Gives us a reason for living.

f. Assures our satisfaction in God and His design for our lives.

g. Helps to keep us organized and more productive. Who couldn't use some help in those areas of life?

Prophetic Insights For Daily Living:

Define your physical and spiritual wheelhouse(s). If you are unsure of them, pray and ask God for He will surely reveal them to you through The Holy Spirit. Both Jesus and The Holy Spirit continue to pray for us even when we don't think They are. (Romans 8:26-27; and 34)

_____
_____
_____

1. Consult with Christian believers, family members, and trusted friends or co-workers for confirmations. All of them may be able to help you evaluate. We may have spread ourselves too thin over the past year without realizing it. Tweaking will solve that problem on several fronts.
2. There's a special, heavenly window of grace and opportunity during the month of February to do this necessary tweaking. The manner in which this will be confirmed to you is that you will not have thought of the necessary adjustments in your own natural thinking process. God has many ways to speak to us. Press in and listen.

3. You're the only one in your wheelhouse, so it's incumbent upon you to do this. The assignment is yours, not someone else's.

God-given connections may suddenly arise to help you complete your assignment. Please be on the lookout for them.

4. This is an exciting opportunity and fun exercise if we can look at it in that regard.

5. I'm starting my assignment this week. To that end, I've drawn a wheelhouse for each of the physical and spiritual ones that The Holy Spirit has quickened unto me. I'm filling those in as He leads and directs. I plan to follow His lead for the necessary tweaks as He helps me to evaluate my life. How must your wheelhouses be tweaked to prepare for 2021 and beyond?

_____

_____

_____

God is our Jehovah-Jireh (Genesis 22:14), and He will provide what we need in our wheelhouses.

I'd love to hear from some of you in blogger-reader land as to how you tweaked your wheelhouses. I'm sure other readers would benefit as well. The rising tide benefits all ships. Happy sailing and tweaking!

Sheila Eismann, Prophetic Seer, Blogger, Author & Teacher, publishes her weekly blog posts endeavoring to encourage others through God's word. Her writings include teaching and instructions on how to apply prophetic insights for daily living. You can subscribe to receive new blog posts on her website at www.sheilaeismann.com.

The Maturity Is In The Waiting

February 16, 2021
Prophetic Words

Do you enjoy spending time in the waiting rooms of doctor's offices, grocery store lines, traffic lanes, or anyplace else? This was probably more applicable during the pre-pandemic days, but I'm sure you can still recall what it was like in former times. For those of us who are hard-wired more like the *Energizer Bunny* or have an administrative gifting, we chafe more against the wait; however, I would like to encourage you with this prophetic word which I received recently, "The maturity is in the waiting." Freedom from anxiety is freedom indeed!

Please tap your personal brakes for a moment, and fill in this line, whether orally or in writing:

"My life would be better if only _____
_____
_____."

Notice I did not use the word **perfect**, but better. Perfection will not exist until we are in heaven with Jesus Christ.

What are your three biggest battles or concerns at this very moment?

#1._____
_____

#2._____
_____

#3._____
_____

Sometimes when we write things down, it helps to alleviate a bit of the pressure and to focus more intently.

I can almost hear some of you out there in blogger-reader land, "Top three? Shake yourself! I've got my *Top Twenty List*."

The reason I suggested only three is because that's easier to bite off at one time than a lengthy anxiety list. Freedom from anxiety should be one of our major goals in life.

Perhaps the most critical factor concerning our battles and concerns is to discern whether it's something that God has instructed us to do or if the matter is completely beyond our control.

If the issue is our sole responsibility or one we've been assigned to help co-labor with, then we must search our hearts to make sure we've done all that we can for the time being.

The more challenging aspect is the case wherein we have no control.

How do you react when things don't go as we planned or when we don't get your way in a situation?

_____
_____
_____
_____

I'm sure all of you have some sort of testimony you could readily render as we continue to flesh out this subject.

On a personal note, I waited, and not so patiently at many times, 23 years for my father to get saved. This was painful and frustrating to walk through as

Daddy was so resistant for many years. Finally, he consented to read a King James Version of the Bible if we gifted it to him.

Once Daddy began reading the Bible, I can still recall phone conversations with him wherein he would call and read me various passages from the Old Testament. He was somewhat horrified as he read about gruesome battles and other things. It was as if he couldn't bring himself to believe those sorts of things were a part of Biblical history; however, one thing the Word of God does afford us is deep insight into some of the world's prior civilizations. To quote our friend, Denno, "Sometimes the truth isn't real pretty, but it's still the truth."

Daddy's personal resistance to accepting Jesus Christ as his personal Lord and Savior before he passed away was his battles during World War II. He thought he could never be forgiven for his actions toward enemy soldiers.

Three weeks before Daddy died, we received a call from the medical facility where he was staying. There was such a sense of urgency to this, that my husband, son, and I dropped everything and headed over to see him. During the course of our visit, my husband gave Daddy the salvation message one more time. This was the appointed day and hour in which he chose to accept Jesus and get saved. It was in the nick of time as within days after this, he had a stroke, could no longer speak, and went to be with Jesus on our 24th wedding anniversary. 24 is symbolic of the priesthood of all believers in the one and only true Jesus Christ of Nazareth. (1 Peter 2:9-10; Revelation 1:6)

The Parable of the Workers in the Vineyard reinforces the point that as long as someone makes it into the vineyard before it closes, he or she is still saved, their name is written in the Lamb's Book of Life, and they will go to heaven. (Matthew 20:1-16)

My book titled *Stirrings of The Spirit* chronicles this true story regarding my dad along with other healings, miracles, dreams, visions, fulfillments of words of knowledge, etc. (1 Corinthians 12:1-11)

What are some aspects that develop or mature in the waiting?

Trust (Proverbs 3:5-6)
Love
Joy (James 1:2-3)
Patience (Romans 15:4; 2 Thessalonians 3:5; Hebrews 6:12)
Longsuffering
Hope
Faith
Our light shines brighter (Matthew 5:16)
We discover a greater dimension of God's grace which is sufficient for us in all circumstances (2 Corinthians 12:9)
Godliness with contentment is great gain (1 Timothy 6:6-10)
The fruits of The Holy Spirit (Galatians 5:22-23)
A deeper prayer life (We prayed for 23 years for my dad before he gave his life to Jesus and got saved)
God's destiny and plans for our lives are fulfilled as we complete our books written for us in heaven.

What could you add to the above list?

_____

_____

_____

_____

Lest we think that people who lived millennia ago did not face the same mountains of maturity, we're kidding ourselves. For a deeper dive, I would encourage you to study the lives of Joseph in the Old Testament and the Apostle Paul in the New Testament. Consider the fruit of their lives once it was in full bloom. Joseph was appointed Prime Minister in Egypt to save the world from starvation during the time of a prolonged famine. Paul wrote two-thirds of the New Testament, some of it while being severely mistreated.

Have you ever taken a short-cut road or path to get to your desired destination only to discover that it was not the wisest choice at the time? It seems as though there are no shortcuts to reaching maturity in our spiritual walks either.

Trying to deal with situations and problems completely out of our control without God's help and His word can lead to much anxiety which affects our overall health in short order.

If the Apostle Paul could pen the following verse while sitting inside a jail cell in Rome, we can take encouragement and sage advice from it:

"Be anxious for nothing, but in everything by prayer and supplication, with thanksgiving, let your requests be made known to God; and the peace of God, which surpasses all understanding, will guard your hearts and minds through Christ Jesus." (Philippians 4:6-7)

Nothing means just that, nothing. It infers that if we are anxious, we rob ourselves of Godly peace which is an inherent safeguard for our hearts and minds. I think we could safely say that The Apostle Paul fully achieved freedom from anxiety.

Anxiety is a two-pronged thief both spiritually and physically. What's it stealing from you?

_____
_____
_____
_____

Please join me in preparing a cup of tea or coffee, sit down to rest, and soothe your soul with these verses regarding anxiety:

(a) Isaiah 35:4

(b) Psalms 55:22; 94:19

(c) Proverbs 12:25

(d) Matthew 6:25, 27, and 34

(e) Luke: 12:25-26

(f) John 14:27

(g) Romans 8:38-39

(h) Philippians 4:13-14

(i) 2 Thessalonians 3:16

(j) Hebrews 13:6

(k) 1 Peter 5:7

How do you feel after meditating upon them? Which verse(s) comforted you, and why?

_____
_____
_____
_____

Isaiah 40:22 instructs us that God sits enthroned above the earth. Implementing His omnipotence, omniscience, and omnipresence, He also sits enthroned **above every situation** in our lives. To say otherwise would infer that He's not in control, and there's someone or something else which is in control. As students of His Word, we know that to be untrue.

The cults espouse that man can become a god. This is why they typically have their own writings which they rank higher than and give more authority to than the word of God. Isaiah 44:6-8 and other Biblical verses assure us there is only one God. We must continue to pray for those in the cults that the veils would be lifted from their hearts, eyes, minds, and spirits to see the true Jesus and accept Him as their personal Lord and Savior before it's too late. They can't get into heaven after the vineyard has closed.

God, His Son, Jesus, and The Holy Spirit work in tandem for us. If God is for us, who can be against us? (Romans 8:31) This is especially important to keep in mind while we're patiently waiting for a situation to be resolved or for maturity to come to fruition where needed. It's important to get Their (The Heavenly Tribunal's) perspective on what we need.

Ask the Heavenly Tribunal as to how They view the issue and what you can and should do about it if anything. To get Their perspective, we've got to stay in communication with Them. This is where fervent prayer enters the picture. Oftentimes, we can be holding onto something so tightly that God has to pry it loose from our fingers. It's much easier to surrender it to Him in the first place.

Once upon a time, I heard a sermon preached with the catchy acronym:

P U S H = Pray Until Something Happens! Holy Spirit-led prayer can lessen anxiety when needed as well. Also, stand on the promises of God in the Bible for what you need. There's great comfort in this.

Speaking of standing on the promises, I'm reminded of Abraham and Sarah waiting for Isaac, their son of the promise. "By faith Abraham, when he was tested, offered up Isaac, and he who had received the promises offered up his only begotten *son*." (Hebrews 11:17-18) Abraham not only received the promise, but he passed the test.

Many years ago, we knew a couple who were involved in a lengthy litigation matter. They lost on the first round but decided to try their case again. As my husband and I continued to pray for them, I received a word from the Lord for them from Exodus 14:13-14, "And Moses said to the people, 'Do not be afraid. Stand still, and see the salvation of the LORD, which He will accomplish for you today. For the Egyptians whom you see today, you shall see again no more forever. The LORD will fight for you, and you shall hold your peace.'"

I contacted the husband and told him what I'd received during my prayer time for them. I asked him to write the verses down on an index card and place it inside his wallet. At that time, they lived in the west and the case was being tried in the east which necessitated many airplane trips back and forth.

This couple wavered and did not stand on the word of the Lord and His promises. Their attorneys were afraid that the decision on a case on appeal to the Supreme Court would end their case. The decision later issued in the appeal would not have affected their case. Consequently, this couple settled for FAR less than the jury had awarded. They did not stand upon the promise of God or His timely word.

Prophetic Insights for Daily Living:

What is God maturing in you?

_____
_____
_____
_____

What promise(s) has He given to you? If you haven't received any, pray and ask Him to give you one or some.

_____
_____
_____
_____

The Bible has a lot to say on the subject of waiting. It would be a great topical or independent study if you feel led to do so the next time you might be feeling anxious about your situation. Write down the corresponding promises relative to your problem, and stand on them!

Before I sign off this week, here's a grandiose promise from God spoken through one of His prophets in Isaiah 40:31,

"But those who wait on the LORD
Shall renew *their* strength;
They shall mount up with wings like eagles,

They shall run and not be weary,
They shall walk and not faint."

Sheila Eismann, Prophetic Seer, Blogger, Author & Teacher, publishes her weekly blog posts endeavoring to encourage others through God's word. Her writings include teaching and instructions on how to apply prophetic insights for daily living. You can subscribe to receive new blog posts on her website at www.sheilaeismann.com.

The Time of Your Life

March 4, 2021
Prophetic Teachings

How many times have you heard the phrase or received an invitation including the words, "The Time of Your Life?" Attend or come to thus and such, and you'll have the time of your life. Also, reflection can cause one to utter, "I had the time of my life when I took a cruise, visited Europe, toured an art museum, catered a birthday party for my neighbor's 7-year-old daughter, etc." While this may quite often apply, this week's blog post addresses the spiritual aspect of the time of your life. I guess one could say there's spiritual time and physical time.

Enter the book of Ecclesiastes which was penned by Solomon, the second king of united Israel, and the wisest man who ever lived other than Jesus Christ of Nazareth. It's conjectured that Solomon wrote this toward the end of his life after repenting of idolatry and marriages to innumerable wives.

To tee up the premise, let's focus upon Ecclesiastes 3:1,

"To everything *there is* a season,
A time for every purpose under heaven:"

These two lines signal three key perspectives which are all intertwined:

A. Season

B. Time

C. Purpose

The remainder of Ecclesiastes 3:2-8 reads,

"A time to be born,
And a time to die;
A time to plant,
And a time to pluck *what is* planted;
A time to kill,

And a time to heal;

A time to break down,

And a time to build up;

A time to weep,

And a time to laugh;

A time to mourn,

And a time to dance;

A time to cast away stones,

And a time to gather stones;

A time to embrace,

And a time to refrain from embracing;

A time to gain,

And a time to lose;

A time to keep,

And a time to throw away;

A time to tear,

And a time to sew;

A time to keep silence,

And a time to speak;

A time to love,

And a time to hate;

A time of war,

And a time of peace."

In the above verses, it's important to realize that each time has a beginning and an ending. None of them last forever. Also, not every one of them is fun and games. For example, a time to mourn.

In addition, there can repetitive ones for some of them excluding a time to be born and a time to die.

Time takes discernment, so we can know what our God-given task or assignment is for right now. Jesus said, "Occupy till I come." (Luke 19:13 KJV)

Part of His command to occupy is to know what time it is and what we're supposed to be doing. Notice this is not an option if you're a Christian and a disciple of Christ. It's a command.

The Greek word for occupy is Strong's G4231 – *Pragmateuoma* which means to be occupied in anything. In other words, we're to be about the Father's business which is the kingdom of God business. This is how we fulfill our destiny. We are to faithfully serve in the kingdom until Jesus calls us home.

https://www.blueletterbible.org/lang/Lexicon/Lexicon.cfm?strongs=G4231&t=KJV

Jesus' command comes from the Parable of the Minas or Talents. (Luke 19:11-27) He expects us to be serving faithfully, and He wants to see dividends or returns on His investment in our lives. We will ultimately have to give an account for what we did with the talents He entrusted to us.

https://sheilaeismann.com/spiritual-puzzle/

Are you putting your talents to good use? In order to do this, you've got to know what time it is. Not only what time it is, but the season of your life.

_____
_____
_____
_____

Seasons can be much more anticipated and somewhat predictable than time.

For instance, there are four seasons in our geographic part of the country. Before winter, there are necessary preparations and precautions which need to be completed such as closing the house vents, winterizing the furnace system, and so forth. When spring rolls around, it's time to spray dormant oil on the trees and shrubs ahead of the leafing stages thereof.

If we have children, the seasons of parenting and grandparenting are totally different.

God has created both times and seasons. He's created them; ergo, He controls them.

Since our lives are to be lived in total subjection to God, we must stay in touch with and walk in lock-step with Him, so we can stay on His timetable. The seasons of our lives can overlap the times of our lives as specified in Ecclesiastes.

An easy example would be Ecclesiastes 3:6b,

"A time to keep,

And a time to throw away;"

The early decades of our lives are typically spent accumulating things for our enjoyment and living every day; however, there comes a time when we need to down-size or decide how to dispose of some of them for obvious reasons. The exception would be the sentimental, important generational items that should and need to be saved for posterity.

From the above example, the season would be as we're wrapping up life here on earth, and the time would be to start sorting through everything we have to determine what to do with it.

In this same passage of scripture from Ecclesiastes 3, verse 4b reads, "A time to mourn."

This can be a more challenging one as everyone grieves in different ways, and there's no exact time frame for this. Yes, grieving is very important and is part of a natural life cycle. If one spends the remainder of his or her days mourning or grieving a loss, the danger is that grief can overtake us, and we can lose our strength.

I would like to share with you the way I've been led by The Holy Spirit the past few weeks regarding this whole business of *The Time of Your Life.* He's instructed me to read very slowly down through the verses of Ecclesiastes 3:1-8. When He stops me at a certain point, I'm to do the following:

Pause
Read the scripture The Holy Spirit is focusing upon
Pray
Record the impartation and other Bible verses I'm given
Reflect upon them
Act and proceed accordingly as I'm directed

An illustration of this would be Ecclesiastes 3:2b, "A time to plant." I might also mention that there can be corresponding physical and spiritual applications to these verses.

Planting could include a natural vegetable or flower garden, placing Bibles inside every pew or on every chair in your church sanctuary, or spiritual seeds of hope when penning a monthly letter to someone who's incarcerated.

DANGER ALERT:

If we're not on God's time for our lives and His timetable, the risk we run is that we miss the time of our visitation from Him.

In Luke 19:44, Jesus warned Israel that they would miss the time of their visitation because they had rejected Him for Who He was. They were looking for a political leader instead of a spiritual one. In 70 A.D., horrible destruction and loss came upon them via the hands of the Roman Emperor, Titus.

Can you locate the verse in Ecclesiastes 3:1-8 which Israel violated much to their detriment? Had they done this one thing; history would have been changed forever.

A second danger alert has to do with God granting His permission which happens during the appointed and ordained times of our lives. With the appointed times, divine permission is granted. When we have permission, we have the full *green light* to proceed accordingly.

For instance, if we're supposed to keep silent about something, but disobey and choose to speak, the results will be negative.

Prophetic Insights for Daily Living Personal Impartations For You:

1. The first 8 verses of Ecclesiastes are God's appointed times during your life, not yours; therefore, you must cooperate with Him. Do any of you recall this line of a song from the beloved *Mr. Rogers*

Neighborhood, "Cooperation makes it happen?" If we're cooperating with God, we're not fighting against Him. We'll never win a battle against God. The awesome thing about God when He signals what time it is in your life is that He deposits a desire within you to fulfill it along with the strategies to complete it. How cool is that?

2. If you don't know exactly what time it is in your life, pray and ask God to show you. Don't assume or presume. He will be faithful to reveal it to you.

_____
_____
_____
_____

3. A time is purposefully tied to a purpose. It's not just random without expectation of fulfillment. You will find your life's purpose when you are walking hand-in-hand with God. This will be confirmed to you in a myriad of ways if you will open your eyes and intentionally look for it.
So many people are frustrated as they don't know what they are supposed to be doing in a spiritual sense. Yes, they have their day jobs or have retired, but true fulfillment comes when we're doing what we're born to do. A

physical job fulfills our physical desires, but our spirits can still be null and void until we make the discovery.

If you don't know what you're destined to do, ask yourself these questions:

"What gives me a sense of satisfaction?"

_____
_____
_____

"What am I passionate about?"

_____
_____
_____
_____

"What is it that makes me come alive and jump for joy?"

_____
_____
_____
_____

As you can probably tell when reading through my various blog posts, I especially enjoy encouraging people through God's word and teaching them how to apply it to their everyday lives.

One of my passions is the prophetic and all of the avenues and aspects of that powerful spiritual dimension.

4. There's an anointing of God's grace upon His appointed times of your life. He provides everything you need to walk this out. Do you desire His grace and anointing?
_____
_____
_____

5. If you miss your time of visitation, you miss out on your life's purpose, mission, and assignment(s).

6. Life can either serve as a good tutor or a painful one. We learn from all of our life's experiences, whether good or bad, and trust God that He never wastes any of them according to Romans 8:28.

Your homework assignment, should you choose to accept it:

After ruminating upon the above-listed impartations, what would you add?
_____
_____
_____

What action is your spirit stirred to take relative to the time of your life?
_____
_____
_____

The verse(s) which spoke to me the loudest from Ecclesiastes 3:1-8 were:
_____
_____
_____
_____

This is what I've felt led to act upon as directed by The Holy Spirit of God:
_____
_____
_____
_____

There's a purpose to be fulfilled in every God ordained time frame. What's my purpose **NOW**?
_____
_____
_____
_____

Jesus loves you, and He desires the very best for your life every day. Your times are in His powerful and loving hands. He's just waiting to show you the time of your life!

Sheila Eismann, Prophetic Seer, Blogger, Author & Teacher, publishes her weekly blog posts endeavoring to encourage others through God's word. Her writings include teaching and instructions on how to apply prophetic insights for daily living. You can subscribe to receive new blog posts on her website at www.sheilaeismann.com.

A Cup of Joy

March 9, 2021
<u>Inspiration</u>

How do you fill your cup with joy?

_____
_____
_____
_____

Do you have certain daily or weekly practices or routines?

What sorts of things bring you joy?

Joy can be tightly paired with comfort which is so important for our overall physical, spiritual, and emotional health.

One vital consideration and something of which to be mindful is what sorts of things drain our cup of joy. Granted, this is going to be different for each one of us. What are these in your life?

Since this blog is going to be short and sweet, pour yourself a nice warm cup of tea or coffee as you meditate and thoughtfully reflect upon the questions that I've asked.

I'd love to hear from some of you in blogger-reader land as to your tried-and-true methods. Since the rising tide benefits all ships, we can all learn good, positive things from one another. This is also called "the one-anothering."

Sheila Eismann, Prophetic Seer, Blogger, Author & Teacher, publishes her weekly blog posts endeavoring to encourage others through God's word. Her writings include teaching and instructions on how to apply prophetic insights for daily living. You can subscribe to receive new blog posts on her website at www.sheilaeismann.com.

Where Is Your Car Parked?

March 17, 2021
Prophetic Visions

The thought did occur to me at the outset of writing this week's blog post that some of you might not even own a car if you live in an area where it's challenging to do so. Perhaps you've chosen to not purchase one. Either way, the question, "Where is your car parked?" has more of a spiritual application rather than a physical one. It can be a real eye-opener!

This blog post is Part I in my "Prophetic Personal Growth Series" which is based upon a shift in the prophetic words, dreams, and visions that I've been given from the Lord which is geared more toward the individual as opposed to countries, cities, entities, and so forth.

In a recent prophetic vision, I saw a parking lot with designated parking spots. The image in this post is the closest one I could find to resemble what I will be conveying even though it does not have parking spot signs.

As The Holy Spirit zoomed into these parking slots, the one He focused upon was **BITTERNESS**. The blue car parked in this space belonged to a woman and was splattered with mud. In this first scene of the vision, it was as if a movie camera filmed other parking spots with the signs reading Anger, Unforgiveness, Hate, and so forth. In a different area of the parking lot were signs bearing the words Love, Hope, Forgiveness, and Joy.

The Spiritual Car Wash

The verse which was quickened unto me comes from Ephesians 5:25-26 which reads, "Husbands, love your wives, just as Christ also loved the church and gave Himself for her, that He might sanctify and cleanse her with the washing of water by the word."

Jesus Christ loved the church so much that He was willing to give His life for believers in Him and sanctify them. When we read the Word of God continually, it's like we take our daily bath or shower. "For the word of God *is* living and powerful, and sharper than any two-edged sword, piercing even to the division of soul and spirit, and of joints and marrow, and is a discerner of the thoughts and intents of the heart." (Hebrews 4:12)

A car is symbolic of a person's life. Mud represents someone who's stuck, backsliding and going back into the world from the kingdom of God, and being without a solid footing or foundation in God. A parked auto means being worked on and a place of preparation.

As the vision continued, this woman didn't fully realize her car was parked in this particular slot or how dirty it was. As she walked, she'd been looking down at the pavement. Suddenly, she looked up and read the black and white sign marking the slot which read **BITTERNESS**.

A small, white cloud appeared above her head which I knew represented revelation from heaven. This showed her how she'd allowed the root of bitterness to grow so deeply within her to where it had become a taproot.

https://en.wikipedia.org/wiki/Taproot

The Warning Against Bitterness

"Pursue peace with all *people,* and holiness, without which no one will see the Lord: looking carefully lest anyone fall short of the grace of God; lest any root of bitterness springing up cause trouble, and by this many become defiled." (Hebrews 12:14-16)

When I read the above verse, it sort of reminds me of one of those red flag alerts companies sometimes float out when they discover a contaminated product and have to recall it. The warning is circulated to protect humanity from adverse effects. Please notice that the above verse from Hebrews 2:14-

16 states that when the root of bitterness springs up, it causes trouble. It's highly contagious!

Bitterness is a lair of cruelty that we may have crawled into without realizing it. The longer we dwell there, the worse it gets and the deeper and stronger the taproot grows. It's a silent, terrible thief. It can come in and steal from us without us being aware of it.

Bitterness and unforgiveness are sort of like the evil twin sisters. The good twin sisters would be sweetness and forgiveness.

Life can dish out many trials, tribulations, and hardships. We can run the risk of becoming bitter without even realizing it. However, just like any other physical taproot which begins to bear fruit, others will quickly notice unpleasant fruit born from bitterness evident in our actions, attitudes, behaviors, and speech.

https://sheilaeismann.com/dream-therapy/

In the ongoing vision, when the woman read the sign, she got inside her car and started sobbing.

Love to The Rescue

In the next scene of the vision, a second woman entered the parking lot on foot which was in a different area than where she'd originally parked. As she walked by, she spotted the woman sitting inside her blue car, holding her face in her hands and crying. She walked to the mud-splattered blue car and motioned for the driver to roll the window down.

While I was not privy to their conversation, the result was the woman in the blue car followed the other woman who walked to her parking spot bearing the sign **LOVE.** True, authentic love changes everything!
Before departing, the woman driving the blue car parked it, got out of her car, and hugged the other woman.

End of vision.

The Three R's

As I've continued to pray into this prophetic vision, *The Three R's* were dropped into my spirit, but they are not the type we learned when I was in grade school which were Reading, Writing, and 'Rithmetic.
The applicable ones here are:

Repentance
Refreshing
Ruth – the book of Ruth in the Bible

Acts 3:19-21, "Repent therefore and be converted, that your sins may be blotted out, so that times of refreshing may come from the presence of the Lord, and that He may send Jesus Christ, who was preached to you before, whom heaven must receive until the times of restoration of all things, which God has spoken by the mouth of all His holy prophets since the world began."

Times of refreshing come after we have truly repented which includes completely turning away from whatever ungodly actions and decisions are applicable in our lives. After doing so, we turn to Jesus Christ, our Healer, and Redeemer.

Refreshing brings restoration, nourishment, and strength which ushers in hope.

The book of Ruth in the Old Testament consists of only four chapters, but they carry the powerful theme of redemption. Naomi, one of the lead characters in the book, has given herself a new name which is *Mara* and the meaning thereof is bitter. (Ruth 1:20) Ironically enough, the meaning of Naomi's name is *The Pleasant One*. It's so encouraging to study how God redeems Naomi and her lineage. Now, that read is a real eye-opener!

Prophetic Insights For Daily Living

Where is your car parked? If you're unsure, pray and ask the Lord Jesus to show you or consult with a trusted, mature believer in Christ.

_____
_____
_____
_____

If your car is parked in a negative spot, repent, and select a spiritually positive one. How we live our daily lives is a basic choice just like everything else we may encounter.

If you've been parked in a spot so long your battery is dead or your car is stalled, Jesus is the perfect One with Whom to connect. The Holy Spirit will give you a jump-start or a whole new battery!

Ask yourself if where you are parked is violating any of God's commands such as, "You shall love your neighbor as yourself." (Romans 13:8-10)

_____
_____
_____
_____

We may have to distance ourselves from some situations or relationships if they contribute to us staying parked in a continually negative spot.

If applicable, calculate what parking in the wrong spot has cost you. Granted, it may seem like there's no parking meter with an expiration timer on it, but bad choices always carry a hefty price tag, both physically and spiritually.

Select a prayer partner or accountability person to help if needed.

A concentrated Bible study on topics such as forgiveness, love, joy, etc. may be in order. You can do an independent study or there is a variety of them online from which you can choose.

The first day of spring is this coming Saturday, March 20th, 2021. God, Jesus, and The Holy Spirit love us and are ever-present to help with whatever we need ~ even if it's washing our cars or the spring cleaning that some of us don't relish!

"But as it is written:

'Eye has not seen, nor ear heard,
Nor have entered into the heart of man
The things which God has prepared for those who love Him.'" (1 Corinthians 2:9)

Sheila Eismann, Prophetic Seer, Blogger, Author & Teacher, publishes her weekly blog posts endeavoring to encourage others through God's word. Her writings include teaching and instructions on how to apply prophetic insights for daily living. You can subscribe to receive new blog posts on her website at www.sheilaeismann.com.

Going Your Own Way

March 26, 2021
Prophetic Dreams

Within the past few weeks, I was given a prophetic vision and a prophetic dream with basically the same theme of *Going Your Own Way*. This is Biblical "twice-speak", so to speak when a message is repeated for emphasis, especially within a short time frame. Inherent within both spiritual messages are the dangers of distractions.

This blog post is Part II in my "Prophetic Personal Growth Series" which is based upon a shift in the prophetic words, dreams, and visions that I've been given from the Lord which is geared more toward the individual as opposed to countries, cities, entities, and so forth.

On February 17, 2021, when the vision opened in the Spirit realm, I saw a woman walking down a hallway with a series of identical white doors. As she walked, this woman looked down at her cell phone the entire time. Without looking up, she opened a door. Suddenly, she went into free-fall into outer, complete darkness. I waited to see if anything else manifested in this vision, but it did not.

End of prophetic vision.

Respectfully, I deem this is a prophetic warning to someone in "blogger-reader land" to look straight ahead and not get distracted. As I write this, I'm reminded of Psalm 16:8, "I have set the Lord always before me; Because *He is* at my right hand I shall not be moved."

Continuing with a theme of 17 here as this vision was given to me on the 17th, my husband and I visited one of the largest cities in our nation in September of 2017. During that time, we walked an average of 7 miles per day up and down the overcrowded city streets. To our sheer astonishment, the vast majority of people we observed, irrespective of age, walked throughout the city in the same manner as this woman did in the vision on February 17, 2021, with their heads looking down at their cell phone screens. In addition, the majority of them had some type of listening device in their ears. There was virtually no way they could see or hear anything other than their self-directed focus.

Prophetic Insights For Daily Living Regarding The Prophetic Vision:

#1. If you or someone you know needs some encouragement, direction, or would like to do a mini-topical Bible Study regarding the issue of distraction, here are some helpful verses:

Proverbs 3:6 and 4:25

Matthew 14:28-31

Mark 1:35; 4:19; and 6:31

Luke 10:38-42

Romans 12:2

1 Corinthians 7:35; 10:13

Ephesians 5:15-16 and 6:11

Colossians 3:1-2

James 4:7

Hebrews 12:2

1 Peter 5:8

1 John 2:15 and 5:21

#2. As you ponder this vision, what sorts of things tend to distract you since some of us may have this challenge?

_____
_____
_____
_____.

#3. The symbolism for a touchscreen cell phone is a person whose heart is sensitive to God and His Spirit; however, just as with anything, there's both a positive and negative connotation.

#4. The prophet Daniel prophesied the technological advancement and rapid acceleration of knowledge throughout the globe in Daniel 12:4, "But you, Daniel, shut up the words, and seal the book until the time of the end; many shall run to and fro, and knowledge shall increase."

#5. It's so easy to fall into (no pun intended) a bad habit of continually looking down at the ground when viewing our cell phone screens and walking. If we continue to practice this, there's no telling what we may fall into!

Early in the morning of March 4th, 2021, and with 4 being symbolic of an open door, I had the following prophetic dream:

Scene #1 of the dream:

An older woman was standing behind a man named Wes. She placed her right hand on the small of his back and felt a cyst that was full of water.

Wes was wearing a black, pin-striped suit, white shirt, and tie. The older woman knew that he needed medical help, so she suggested he go to her local doctor. There was a second woman in the dream who was younger than Wes and the older woman.

Symbolism for 1st scene:

1. A suit represents a business, pastor, desire for prominence (expensive suit, and this was an expensive suit that Wes was wearing in the dream).

2. Doctor is symbolized by Jesus, authority, Holy Spirit balm, sickness, the need for medication, and the need to seek God for healing.

3. In the dream, Wes had a cyst on his back. Symbolisms for back are past, reverse, behind, return, burden, persistent, or secret exit.

4. The meaning of Wes' name is a major clue in this dream:

"Literal Meaning: West Field

Suggested Character Quality: Prosperous Spirit

Suggested Lifetime Scripture Verse: Psalm 13:6, "I will sing to the Lord, because He has dealt bountifully with me."

Explanation: Those names which have to do with fields, meadows, or land suggest prosperity."

Scene #2 of the dream:

In the next scene of the dream, Wes and the two women were walking single file. Suddenly, both women turned right and walked down a flight of stairs. The older woman didn't realize it at the time, but Wes kept walking straight.

When both women arrived in the downstairs area, it was dark with a party atmosphere. They went to the corner to purchase something. Everything that was being sold seemed to have a milk chocolate theme to it.

Suddenly, when the older woman returned to the booth where she'd been sitting, throngs of people were crammed inside the booth, and she could not find her fanny pack or reading glasses.

After searching for a little bit, she found her fanny pack. Her heart started to race as she unzipped the various compartments of the fanny pack. She was horrified and saddened that her wallet with her driver's license and credit cards had been stolen. Also, she'd lost her reading glasses without which she could barely function or read. The older woman tried to locate some type of phone to call for help but was unsuccessful in doing so.

The interesting thing about this scene of the dream is that the older woman did not have a cell phone with her. Compare this to the woman in the vision who never took her eyes off her cell phone. It's just an interesting thought.

Symbolism for 2nd scene:

1. Stairs (going down) represent stairway to death, going away from God, self-indulgence, being seduced away from God, loss of heart, and becoming progressively more ungodly.
2. Party atmosphere speaks for itself and needs no interpretation for symbolism.
3. Chocolate, which in this case would probably have more of a negative representation since it was in a dark, party atmosphere symbolizes money-hungry, hungry for pleasure, self-indulgence, or sweet, deceptive words.
4. Older woman lost her wallet and credit cards which symbolize her identity and earthly navigation.
5. Reading glasses without which the older woman could not function daily represents learning, teaching, understanding, meditation, receiving revelation, and spiritual conviction.

Scene #3 of the dream:

In this last scene of the prophetic dream, it was as if the older woman was supernaturally lifted 20 feet high and could lean against the wall to see the chaos inside the room.

Then the older woman realized Wes had followed the straight and narrow path. I don't know if he ended up at a doctor's office or not because the dream ended before this.

Symbolism for 3rd scene:

20 (feet high) is symbolic of redemption, expectancy, waiting, accountability, responsibility, and service.

End of prophetic dream.

Prophetic Insights For Daily Living Regarding The Prophetic Dream:

#1. In reality, nothing's really changed from the days of Adam and Eve living in the garden who ultimately decided they wanted to live an autonomous lifestyle. What was the end result? Read all about it in the 3rd chapter of Genesis. Since man is born with a sinful nature (Romans 5:12), there will always be that temptation lurking somewhere, even after we've given our lives to Jesus Christ (Romans 10:9-10) and made Him Lord of our lives (John 14:23-24).

#2. There's obviously a stark contrast between the actions of the people in the prophetic vision and the prophetic dream. As you ponder both of them, what insights, revelation, scriptures, and cautions or warnings come to you?

_____
_____
_____
_____.

#3. Based upon the theme of the meaning of Wes' name which is prosperous spirit, even if he was headed to the doctor in the dream, if we choose to follow Jesus, it's a far better choice than the direction the two women in the dream chose.

#4. Choices have consequences, some of which are short-term, but the majority of them are long-term.

#5. What are some not-so-obvious repercussions from the dangers of distractions?

_____
_____

Revisiting this blog post on forsaking foolishness and living might be a helpful suggestion as well.

https://sheilaeismann.com/forsake-foolishness/

Life's been ultra-challenging and tumultuous during the days of the Corona Crud, so this time frame lends itself to the dangers of distractions and temptations with all sorts of shiny lures dangling from the enemy's fishing pole. Can any of you relate to this, and if so, how?

Let's pray, shall we? Father, I thank You for this prophetic dream and prophetic vision to hopefully serve as a reminder for all of us to stay on the straight and narrow path spoken of by Your precious Son, Jesus, in Matthew 7: 13-14. Also, thank You for the angels which You've assigned to each one of us to help us along our way. (Matthew 18:10) Teach us to be wise in selecting our friends and the places we traverse. (1 Corinthians 15:33) Help us to place our hand inside Your loving one every day as we're led by Your Holy Spirit.

In the mighty name of Jesus, Amen!

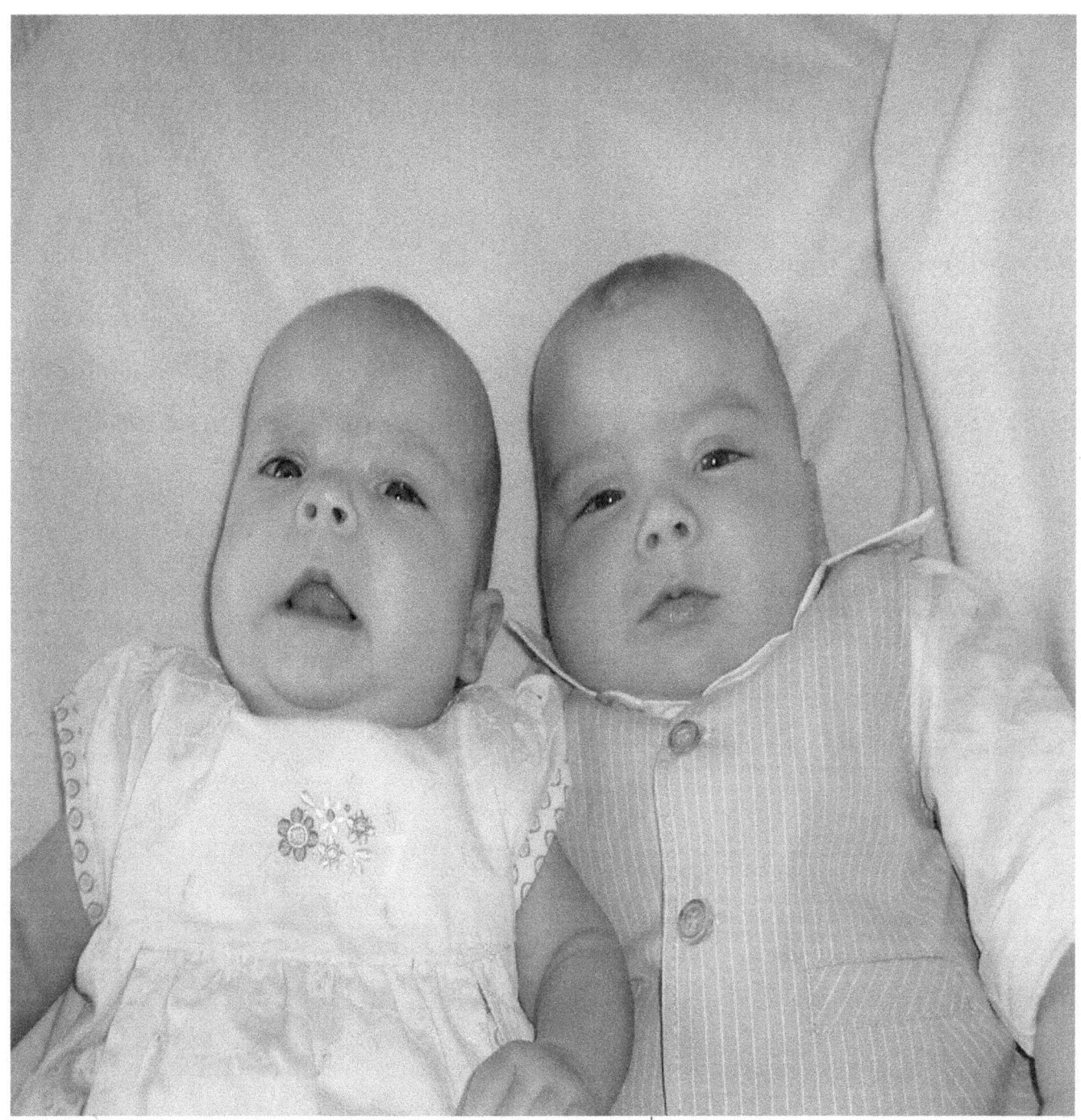

Prophetic Dream – Preferential Treatment

March 31, 2021
Prophetic Dreams

A couple had a set of fraternal twins. From the moment they were born, the husband much preferred one over the other. In fact, it was as if some of the time, one of the twins didn't even exist. The father favored the boy fraternal twin who was "born first," if you will, by a couple of minutes. His extremism took preferential treatment to a whole new level.

Such was the scenario in the prophetic dream which I received on March 28th, 2021. I was not given the man's name nor did I ever talk to him or his wife in this dream.

This blog post is Part III in my "Prophetic Personal Growth Series" which is based upon a shift in the prophetic words, dreams, and visions that I've been given from the Lord which is geared more toward the individual as opposed to countries, cities, entities, and so forth.

Even though I was in a deep sleep, I could feel myself becoming highly irritated with this man. He lived as if he had only one child instead of the two the Lord had given them. The scenes of the dream were repetitive which I deem is for the purposes of emphasis and reinforcement.

End of dream.

In prophetic symbolism, twins represent contention, double-mindedness, a repeat experience, or double blessing or portion.

Do you think preferential treatment is fair? What say you?

_____

_____

_____

_____

In real life, we know a set of fraternal twins. The mother vastly favored the boy who was born just a few minutes before his sister. It was painful to observe how she was treated during their childhood years. Even though she's a grown adult, the girl twin still bears the horrendous emotional and social scars of her mother's preferential treatment toward her brother. It continues to this day.

The sad and unfortunate thing is that this wounded girl twin scarred other people in her life. Wounded people often wound others. If we've been treated in this manner during our lifetime, we can draw near to our Healer, Jesus. He can heal our hearts, but He has to be given all of the pieces to do so.

Family Dynamics

In some families, perhaps some of us can reflect and say that _____ was our father's favorite or that our mother favored _____. This can apply to grandchildren as well.

Parenting can be a supreme challenge at best whether our children are natural-born, adopted, or step-children.

Blended families come with inherent obstacles and dimensions that may not surface in a natural one.

From Fractured to Blended

But if we can look at it in this manner, all of us are born into sin and could be tagged or labeled as "a fractured family" until we accept Jesus Christ as our personal Lord and Savior. It's at that point that we're adopted into the kingdom of God as sons and daughters. (Ephesians 1:5) Talk about a big, blended family!

If we think we get frustrated as parents and grandparents, consider how God must feel. Implementing some country-western vernacular, He has to "ride herd" on a whole bunch of people simultaneously.

Under the Old Covenant, the first-born son was given a double portion of his father's inheritance. (Deuteronomy 21:17) There's the landmark portion of the Bible wherein Isaac's oldest son, Esau, sells his birthright for a bowl of soup. The significance of this is that when Isaac graduated to heaven, Esau was destined to get all of his land, money, and possessions until he made a very unwise choice. Anyone can realize this is a trade deal gone bad in a hurry. However, it was to fulfill a prophecy in Genesis 25:22-24.

In some instances and cultures, when a person becomes a born-again Christian, he or she is immediately carved off from their family. God comes to the rescue once again as the Psalmist reminds us in Psalm 68:6.

As you're reading through this message, perhaps some of you may think it's quite far-fetched that a parent would show such preferential treatment; someone is carved off for a true, Biblical spiritual choice; or that such extremes exist in familial situations. However, it is applicable in some cases. Can any of you relate?

_____
_____
_____
_____

In addition, are any of you an identical twin or a fraternal twin? If so, what's your input?

_____
_____
_____
_____

The Church in Jerusalem

Another layer to this is the spiritual dimension where people can be treated differently in church settings. In light of this, I wonder what was happening in the church in Jerusalem to cause the Apostle James to pen a note of caution and correction in James 2:1-7? For him to even mention it and the verses printed in the canon of scripture, do you think people would have been operating in this manner?

Prophetic Insights For Daily Living:

As you reflect upon the man in the dream and how he viewed his set of twins, what are your thoughts, and what scriptures are quickened unto you?

_____
_____
_____
_____

During the time that you were reading this blog post, did it stir up old wounds and emotions in your heart and mind that still need to be healed?

_____
_____
_____
_____

While I can't speak to other countries and cultures, the thought has occurred to me several times that in our country, we have a type of "caste system" of sorts. There can be a dangerous tendency to "rate" people commensurate with their vocation or status. In prior years when speaking at Women's Conferences, I would gently remind those in attendance that God looks at the grocery store clerk in the same light as the CEO of a major corporation. Say what? All of mankind is created in God's image. We see this when the heavenly tribunal, i.e., God, Jesus, and The Holy Spirit give us a bird's eye view in Genesis 1:26.

God is looking for the end result or long game in our lives. First and foremost, have we accepted His Son, Jesus Christ, as our personal Lord and

Savior, so our name is written in the Lamb's book of life? (Luke 10:20, Philippians 4:3 and Revelation 20:11-15)

Are you someone who's been attacked by another person who's infected with the spirit of jealousy? (Numbers 5:14) An example of this would be that pretend you don't have a Ph.D. in a given area or are not a high-ranking member of a corporation and have been looked down upon or spurned in any way. **Please understand that I'm not casting aspersions upon anyone irrespective of where they are in life. I'm merely using an example to reinforce a point regarding a prophetic dream.**

___

___

___

___

Back to the main point, which is the man in the dream showing preferential treatment to one of his twins, prophetic messages via prophetic words, dreams and visions are delivered to serve as spiritual checkpoints and evaluations.

Let's make some promising, prophetic declarations, shall we?

#1. I am created in the image of God. (Genesis 1:26)

#2. I am loved by God, Jesus, and The Holy Spirit. (Jeremiah 33:3; Romans 5:8, 8:37-39; and 1John 4:9-11)

#3. God is no respecter of persons, and in His eyes, there's no one better or more highly favored than me. (Acts 10:34; Romans 2:12; and Galatians 2:6)

#4. God has definite and wonderful plans for my life. (Jeremiah 29:11)

#5. My book(s) of destiny is in heaven, and I plan to fulfill them with God's help. (Daniel 7:10; Psalm 139:16; 1 Corinthians 13:11-15; and Ephesians 1:11; 2:10; and 4:1)

https://sheilaeismann.com/prepare/

#6. (If applicable) God, I ask You for forgiveness if I've shown preferential treatment to mankind. Please re-align my thought processes to Your word which is truth. (John 17:17)

#7. I choose to have a humble, teachable heart, so I do not stir up strife. (Proverbs 28:25)

#8. I choose to forgive everyone, so my prayers are not hindered. (Psalm 66:18-19; Matthew 6:15; and 1 Peter 3:7)

#9. I am filled with God's love, so I desire to live in God's love and love one another. (John 15:9,17)

#10. (If applicable) God, I thank you for my child(ren) who are my reward(s) from You. "Behold, children *are* a heritage from the Lord, the fruit of the womb *is* a reward. Like arrows in the hand of a warrior, so *are* the children of one's youth." (Psalm 127:3-4)

This prophetic dream was given to me on the 28th day of March 2021. Twenty-eight is symbolic of awaiting or expecting a new beginning. In light of this, my main takeaway from reading this message is:

_____
_____
_____
_____

Even though this is a very short dream regarding a set of fraternal twins, The Holy Spirit stirred my spirit to share it with you. This could be because there's someone who's suffering from the negative effects of preferential treatment. God wants to encourage all of our hearts that He's no respecter of persons.

In between Psalm Sunday and Resurrection Sunday, may you experience God's love, Jesus' presence, and the ministry of The Holy Spirit in a greater way than ever before! Jesus died on the cross for all of humanity. (1 John 2:2)

"But if the Spirit of Him who raised Jesus from the dead dwells in you, He who raised Christ from the dead will also give life to your mortal bodies through His Spirit who dwells in you." (Romans 8:11)

The Woman, The Wishing Well & 1932

April 5, 2021
Prophetic Visions

On the 1st day of April 2021, the Spirit realm opened, and I saw a woman standing beside a wishing well in a garden setting. She released the handle on the bucket which caused it to drop inside the well. When she cranked the rope to bring the bucket to the surface, a bright, red number 2 appeared inside the bucket. She frowned, sat down on the bench by the side of the wishing well, and began to cry. I could feel her sadness and disappointment within my spirit. A blonde-haired angel, wearing a white robe, burgundy sash, and brown leather sandals, approached her holding a Bible with a white cover. The page was turned to The Parable of the Talents. (Matthew 25:14-30)

The angel's finger traced the lines of scripture and stopped on the word "two" as he handed her an antique, white handkerchief to dry her eyes. The Holy Spirit zoomed into the lower right-hand corner of the hankie. 1932 was embroidered thereon.

The angel never did speak to the woman in this vision. (Hebrews 1:14)

I saw a vial of amber-colored liquid appear above the woman's head which represents revelation knowledge from God. This was supernaturally poured into her mind. Her eyes brightened.

This blog post is Part IV in my "Prophetic Personal Growth Series" which is based upon a shift in the prophetic words, dreams, and visions that I've been given from the Lord which is geared more toward the individual as opposed to countries, cities, entities, and so forth.

1 Samuel 14:24-27 flashed through my spirit, "And the men of Israel were distressed that day, for Saul had placed the people under oath, saying, 'Cursed *is* the man who eats *any* food until evening before I have taken vengeance on my enemies.' So none of the people tasted food. Now all *the people* of the land came to a forest; and there was honey on the ground. And when the people had come into the woods, there was the honey, dripping; but no one put his hand to his mouth, for the people feared the oath. But Jonathan had not heard his father charge the people with the oath; therefore he stretched out the end of the rod that *was* in his hand and dipped it in a honeycomb, and put his hand to his mouth; and his countenance brightened."

As the woman continued to sit on the bench, she slowly read the Parable of the Talents aloud. When she got to the word **ability**, The Holy Spirit stopped her. Then her eyes opened even wider which resulted in her downward turned facial muscles now appearing upward as sunbeams streamed through the oak tree behind her.
After reading the parable three times, the woman nodded her head affirmatively.

I heard in the Spirit, "Go your way, and concentrate on the **ability** I have entrusted to you. I'm no respecter of persons. Keep your eyes on Me and not on the numbers."
End of vision.

For a helpful companion read, last week's blog post also aids with the subject of not comparing ourselves to others. (2 Corinthians 10:12) https://sheilaeismann.com/fraternal-twins/

Aspects of Ability

Dynamis, the Greek word for ability, is Strong's G1411 which has several different applications in scripture.

"1. strength power, ability

A. inherent power, power residing in a thing by virtue of its nature, or which a person or thing exerts and puts forth

B. power for performing miracles

C. moral power and excellence of soul

D. the power and influence which belong to riches and wealth

E. power and resources arising from numbers

F. power consisting in or resting upon armies, forces, hosts"

The definition from "A" above applies to Matthew 25:14-30. Inference tells us it's The Holy Spirit residing within us Who supplies the inherent (dynamis) power to help us exert and put forth the effort to gain more talents after we've been entrusted with the original ones. (Matthew 25:21, 23)

https://www.blueletterbible.org/lang/Lexicon/Lexicon.cfm?strongs=G1411&t=KJV

Notice in the Parable of the Talents, the servant stated, "I have gained . . ." (Matthew 25:20) He put forth the required effort after he'd been endowed by the *dynamis* power of the Lord. He didn't let his talents sit idle or bury them in his backyard.

Rivers Launch The Rewards

The parable highlighted in this prophetic vision is teaching about the kingdom of heaven which is within us. (Luke 17:21) Since it's within us, we've been entrusted with the responsibility to accomplish it.

The **reward** is the same, irrespective of the **number** of the talent(s). "So he who had received five talents came and brought five other talents, saying, 'Lord, you delivered to me five talents; look, I have gained five more talents besides them.' His lord said to him, 'Well *done,* good and faithful servant; you were faithful over a few things, I will make you ruler over many things. Enter into the joy of your lord.' He also who had received two talents came and said, 'Lord, you delivered to me two talents; look, I have gained two more talents besides them.' His lord said to him, 'Well *done,* good and faithful servant; you have been faithful over a few things, I will make you ruler over many things. Enter into the joy of your lord.'" (Matthew 25:20-23) As I've continued to pray into this vision, The Holy Spirit has stirred me to shift from a wishing well to a river. John 7:38 is the launchpad, "He who believes in Me, as the Scripture has said, out of his heart will flow rivers of living water."

The Holy Spirit will fuel believers with yielded, obedient hearts to serve God, Who in turn will increase their rewards. Unlike the woman in the vision who let the bucket down into the well where the water is not moving, we have rivers of living water flowing from inside of us. Wishing wells do not launch the rewards. Rivers do which will cause us to jump for joy! (Matthew 25:23)

The number 32, Jeremiah 32, and 1932

This was a really fascinating aspect to this prophetic vision regarding the year 1932 appearing in the lower right-hand corner of the antique, white handkerchief.

The number 100 represents children of the promise and 32 symbolizes covenant.

Jeremiah 32:40-41 speaks of God's covenant with Judah after He instructed His prophet to buy a field, pray for understanding, and assured Him of the return of His people.

"And I will make an everlasting covenant with them (the people of Judah), that I will not turn away from doing them good; but I will put My fear in their hearts so that they will not depart from Me. Yes, I will rejoice over them to do them good, and I will assuredly plant them in this land, with all My heart and with all My soul.'"

1932 was a very pivotal year in American history which saw Franklin D. Roosevelt defeat incumbent Herbert Hoover in a landslide. I would invite you to do some research on this. Irrespective of what happens in the political realm, God will keep His covenant with us to help us fulfill our destiny and increase our talents for His kingdom as we exercise our due diligence and ability from Him.

For those of you who desire to dig a little deeper and do some prophetic homework, consult your ancestral trees. There might be a nugget of encouragement in there concerning a family member who implemented his or her ability to receive rewards even amid very troubling and challenging times in the years following 1932. Record anything The Holy Spirit quickens unto you.

Prophetic Insights For Daily Living:

A portion of this prophetic message is an encouragement to continue to obey God and His word along with staying the course.

Each believer in Jesus is given a different number of talents commensurate with his or her ability.

You'll have a passion that goes with your natural ability which will come with a certain amount of ease and familiarity.

God works out His will for your life through the desires He's divinely placed within your heart. These desires are tied to your ability and talent.

God divinely distributes the ability. We don't choose it.

What abilities has He given to you? Some are more readily discernable than others.

_____
_____
_____
_____

If you're unsure, pray, and God will continue to show you.

Seek spiritual assistance from trusted spiritual sources if necessary.

Look for confirmations and record them. The written record will help to serve as encouragement.

You will be given scriptures by The Holy Spirit as assurance regarding your ability and talent. Record these also. This is where prophetic journaling can really be a good practice.

_____
_____
_____
_____

Even if our ability and talents bear a small amount of fruit at the very beginning of our Christian walk, we must stay encouraged. It's the enemy of our souls who wants us to stay in a state of discouragement.

Ability and talent will always bear good fruit, otherwise, how would we receive a reward in the end?

_____
_____
_____
_____

Back to the woman at the wishing well – don't wish for something that's not been entrusted to you or that you've not been given the ability to do. That would be like chasing a false reward.

Sailing Along With The Spring Breeze

If you are one whose talents are currently producing rewards, Hallelujah! Consider offering a hand up to someone who may be struggling in this area, so you can both sail along with the spring breeze, thus fulfilling Matthew 25:23 wherein you can both enter into the joy of the Lord!

Sheila Eismann, Prophetic Seer, Blogger, Author & Teacher, publishes her weekly blog posts endeavoring to encourage others through God's word. Her writings include teaching and instructions on how to apply prophetic insights for daily living. Please subscribe to receive new blog posts on her website at www.sheilaeismann.com. by clicking the "Subscribe" button in the far upper right-hand corner of her Home webpage.

An Eruption of Miracles

April 9, 2021
Prophetic Words

Much has been written and prophesied of late regarding this being the season of miracles. We've just celebrated and testified of the resurrection of Jesus on 04/04/2021. This date represents double 4's which is symbolic of creation, worldwide, universal, an open door (Revelation 4:1), rule or dimension, the spirit realm, and the 4th man in the fiery furnace, Jesus Christ, as referenced in Daniel Chapter 3. On Friday, April 9, 2021, I heard in the Spirit, "An eruption of miracles." Let's marry miracles up with cancel culture and spring cleaning, shall we?

While every day holds the possibility of miracles, there are definite times and seasons in God's calendar where there seems to be more of a prevalence of them.

This blog post is Part V in my "Prophetic Personal Growth Series" which is based upon a shift in the prophetic words, dreams, and visions that I've been given from the Lord which is geared more toward the individual as opposed to countries, cities, entities, and so forth.

In a recent vision, I saw what resembled an eruption of "Old Faithful," the famous Yellowstone Geyser. In the Spirit, the word **MIRACLES** appeared in dark blue ink at the very tip of the white column.

Here's a brief explanation of what happens to cause the steam one can see when visiting the site.

"Seismic records show that under the **Yellowstone** geyser, a large egg-shaped chamber is connected to the mouth of **Old Faithful** by a sort of pipe.

After every eruption, water levels rise **in** the chamber and send steam **bubbles** into the conduit—which creates a "**bubble** trap" that leads to the eventual steam explosion."

https://www.google.com/search?q=what+bubbles+up+out+of+Old+Faithful&rlz=1C1CHBF_enUS800US801&oq=what+bubbles+up+out+of+Old+Faithful&aqs=chrome..69i57.5438j0j7&sourceid=chrome&ie=UTF-8

There's a play on words of sorts in this as God could well be considered "Old Faithful."

Miracles have been "erupting" and will continue to do so during this season. They'll be much more spectacular to watch than the Yellowstone Geyser. Hallelujah!

The Acts of The Apostles

Reading Acts Chapters 3 through 5 can be a great faith builder when praying and contending for the needed miracles among us. This account details the miraculous healing of the lame man via the hands of Peter and John who ultimately ended up in the clink. (Acts 4:3; 5:17-18)

During a recent study of this passage of scripture, Acts 4:13 leaped off the page into my spirit.

"Now when they saw the boldness of Peter and John, and perceived that they were uneducated and untrained men, they marveled. And they realized that they had been with Jesus."

I was especially struck by two things:

#1. To much of the known world at that time, the apostles were considered uneducated and untrained men.

#2. There was no way to deny that even though they were considered uneducated and untrained, they'd been with Jesus.

I have a rhetorical question for readers, please:

"Is there any one person on the face of the earth who's educated and trained in everything?" Well, of course not. How absurd!

More importantly, the disciples answered the call of God on their lives and spent time with their Lord and Savior, Jesus Christ.

I would like to bless all of you with a much-needed word of encouragement. Continue to follow Jesus with all of your heart; spend time with Him; stay in the center of His will; make yourself available to Him every day; and watch what happens! He is no respecter of persons.

https://sheilaeismann.com/the-parable-of-the-talents/

The Pharisees & Sadducees Among Us

Boy howdy, there's never a shortage of these types around us, is there?

_____

_____

_____

As we continue to set the atmosphere by faith for the miracles to occur, be prepared for the scoffers and naysayers when the miracles manifest. (Acts 4:1-2; 5-7: 5:17)

However, if given the chance, be prepared to testify just as Peter did in Acts 3:17-26 as we must always be prepared to give an answer for the hope that lies within us. (1 Peter 3:15)

Focusing upon the naysayers drains the necessary belief, faith, and obedience for miracles to occur.

Spiritual Spring Cleaning

Just as the natural and spiritual cycles mirror one another, this spring is no different. Many women choose to do a thorough, spring cleaning. Some accomplish this before Passover.

Since The Holy Spirit will not compete with other demonic spirits, He's on the move to do His own type of "house cleaning" during this miraculous season.

Purpose and be intentional to believe, pray into, and record the confirmations of His deep work in delivering people from the following spirits:

spirit of jealousy (Numbers 5:14)

spirit of divination and familiar spirits (1 Samuel 28:7-8)

lying spirit (2 Chronicles 18:22)

spirit of haughtiness (Proverbs 16:18-19)

perverse spirit (Isaiah 19:14)

spirit of heaviness (Isaiah 61:3)

spirit of harlotry (Hosea 4:12)

deaf and dumb spirit (Mark 9:25-26

spirit of infirmity (Luke 13:11)

spirit of bondage (Romans 8:15)

spirit of fear (2 Timothy 1:7)

antichrist spirit (1 John 4:3)

Let's rejoice in John 8:36, "Therefore if the Son makes you free, you shall be free indeed."

Acts 5:29 will cancel Acts 4:17

To say that cancel culture is rapidly on the increase is a mild understatement.

Following the miraculous healing of the lame man in Acts 3, the priests, captain of the temple, and Sadducees were highly irritated.

"Now when they saw the boldness of Peter and John, and perceived that they were uneducated and untrained men, they marveled. And they realized that they had been with Jesus. And seeing the man who had been healed standing with them, they could say nothing against it. But when they had commanded them to go aside out of the council, they conferred among themselves, saying, 'What shall we do to these men? For, indeed, that a notable miracle has been done through them *is* evident to all who dwell in Jerusalem, and we cannot deny *it*. But so that it spreads no further among the people, let us severely threaten them, that from now on they speak to no man in this name.'" (Acts 4:13-17)

We're entering a time when mentioning the name of Jesus in our nation will greatly increase threats against us. (Acts 4:17)

"But Peter and the *other* apostles answered and said: "We ought to obey God rather than men." (Acts 5:29)

I guess you could say the apostles had their own version of "cancel culture" about 2,000 years ago!

Prophetic Insights For Daily Living

1. Pray for an increase and release of The Holy Spirit Gift of Working of Miracles. (1 Corinthians 12:10)

2. Rid yourself of all unbelief. If necessary, pray and ask Jesus to increase your faith as His disciples did. (Luke 17:5-10)

3. Miracles testify of Jesus and cause the unsaved to realize that we've been with Him. (Acts 4:13)

4. True miracles cannot be denied. (Acts 4:14) Have you or someone you know ever experienced a God-given miracle? If so, what was it, and how did it impact your life?

_____
_____
_____
_____

5. Some unbelievers will accept Jesus Christ as their personal Lord and Savior and come unto the kingdom after witnessing a miracle.

Acts 5:12 is a major key for miracles. The apostles were all in one accord.

6. Meditate upon Psalm 133 as the Lord **commands** the blessing when there's unity.

7. Agree in prayer with another believer for whatever miracle you may need. "For where two or three are gathered together in My name, I am there in the midst of them." (Matthew 18:20)

As you're worshipping God, give Him your impossible list. See what He does with it! (Matthew 19:26)

Prophetic Declarations

"I may be uneducated and untrained in many things, **BUT**, I have spent time with Jesus." (Acts 4:13)

How has this blog post ministered to you and what scriptures have spoken to you in a new and encouraging manner?
_____
_____
_____
_____

Let's pray, shall we?

"Now, Lord, look on their threats, and grant to Your servants that with all boldness they may speak Your word, by stretching out Your hand to heal, and that signs and wonders may be done through the name of Your holy Servant Jesus." (Acts 4:29-30)

Sheila Eismann, Prophetic Seer, Blogger, Author & Teacher, publishes her weekly blog posts endeavoring to encourage others through God's word. Her writings include teaching and instructions on how to apply prophetic insights for daily living. Please subscribe to receive new blog posts on her website at www.sheilaeismann.com. by clicking the "Subscribe" button in the far upper right-hand corner of her Home webpage.

Knitting Together God's Plans

April 14, 2021
Prophetic Words

Several sets of hands holding light blue, matching knitting needles appeared in the Spirit. Next, I heard a clicking sound. The hands would knit for a few minutes and stop. Then they would start again. The sense I had was the knitting pertained to corporate, intercessory prayer wherein the intercessors were being given downloads or burdens to pray simultaneously as they were knitting together God's plans. There's a clarion call to action as not everything is as it currently appears.

This blog post is Part VI in my "Prophetic Personal Growth Series" which is based upon a shift in the prophetic words, dreams, and visions that I've been given from the Lord which is geared more toward the individual as opposed to countries, cities, entities, and so forth.

The symbolism for knitting speaks for itself which is uniting, joining, holding together, and woven together with love. As the Spirit zoomed into the needles, I saw the number 7 on each one of them which represents completion, maturity, fullness, promise, and blessings.

The clicking sound reminded me of a telegraph sending out Morse Code. "Developed in the 1830s and 1840s by Samuel Morse (1791-1872) and other inventors, the telegraph revolutionized long-distance communication. It worked by transmitting electrical signals over a wire laid between stations. In addition to helping invent the telegraph, Samuel Morse developed a code (bearing his name) that assigned a set of dots and dashes to each letter of the English alphabet and allowed for the simple transmission of complex messages across telegraph lines. . . . [O]perators were able to hear and understand the code just by listening to the clicking of the receiver."

https://www.history.com/topics/inventions/telegraph

I received this prophetic vision on April 6, 2021, which is just shy of 177 years ago since the advent of the Morse Code.

Scene #2 of the vision opened with seven, large storage buildings that looked like barns with a large loft where yarn was stored. Barns speak of harvest or increase. These barns were sitting on top of 7 mountains.

Here's triple 7's: the knitting needles were a size 7, and 7 barns sat on top of 7 mountains. This totals 21 which is symbolic of fullness, completion, spiritual perfection, serving God, and expecting God. This is a perfect picture for the year 2021.

In the third scene of this vision, I was taken into an expansive room that had a large, oval table in the center of it. There was a circle of tall, rectangular-shaped windows all the way around the room. Stationed against the walls were electronic machines resembling computers except they were not plugged into normal electrical outlets. Different colors of yarn were dispensed from the large barns and fed supernaturally through these machines to the intercessors who were holding their knitting needles.

A map of the United States was spread across the table. Different colors of yarn were stretched completely across the map crisscrossing each other. I saw no chairs anywhere.

End of prophetic vision.

7 Mountain Assignments - ROYGBIV

There's a different color of heavenly issued yarn for each of the 7 mountains of culture, society, and influence. The yarns symbolize the colors of the rainbow representing God's promise. ROYGBIV is the acronym for the colors of the rainbow which are red, orange, yellow, green, blue, indigo, and violet.

In this prophetic vision, I saw these colored yarns streaming from the following 7 mountains:

#1. Religion – Blue

#2. Family – Yellow

#3. Education – Orange

#4. Government – Indigo

#5. Media – Red

#6. Arts & Entertainment – Violet

#7. Business – Green

God is knitting His plans together for each of these mountains irrespective of what it may look like in the natural. I heard in the Spirit, "Not everything is as it currently appears."

The Prayer of The Persistent Widow

The prayer of the persistent widow was quickened unto me.

"Then He (Jesus) spoke a parable to them, that men always ought to pray and not lose heart, saying: 'There was in a certain city a judge who did not fear God nor regard man. Now there was a widow in that city; and she came to him, saying, 'Get justice for me from my adversary.' And he would not for a while; but afterward he said within himself, 'Though I do not fear God nor regard man, yet because this widow troubles me I will avenge her, lest by her continual coming she weary me.'

Then the Lord said, 'Hear what the unjust judge said. And shall God not avenge His own elect who cry out day and night to Him, though He bears long with them? I tell you that He will avenge them speedily. Nevertheless, when the Son of Man comes, will He really find faith on the earth?'" (Luke 18:1-8)

Unlike the unjust judge in this parable, Jesus is our Judge, and He cares to the utmost about what concerns us and our nation. God answers prayer in

His way and in His time. In the interim, as we remain persistent and steadfast, our faith continues to grow in Him. (Mark 11:22-24)

https://sheilaeismann.com/prophetic-dream-2-featuring-silver-coins/

Prophetic Insights For Daily Living

There's a double play on words with double-clicking that I heard which is the clicking of the knitting needles and the clicking sound of Morse Code.

Here are some examples of intercessory prayer:

Genesis 18:20-33

Joshua 7:6-9

Daniel 9:3-5

John 17:1-7

Colossians 1:9-12

1. God is desiring for His church to be knit together in love. Ephesians 4:16, "from whom the whole body, joined and knit together by what every joint supplies, according to the effective working by which every part does its share, causes growth of the body for the edifying of itself in love."
2. After reading this blog post, why do you think that connected, intercessory prayer appeared the way it did in this vision?

_____
_____
_____
_____

3. God is also wanting us to partner with Him to usher radical change and transformation in each of the 7 mountains on all 7 of His continents.

Sudden Violet Confirmations

As The Holy Spirit was helping me write this blog post, these events literally happened:

#1. I saw a man wearing an expensive suit with violet-colored accents and a solid-colored, violet tie. This was a very striking clothing ensemble.

#2. Just last evening, I heard a woman exclaim, "I just started knitting!" I looked down at her **blue knitting needles**, and she was using violet-colored yarn.

#3. I visited a nursery to select some flowers for my patio pots. I saw a sea of violet-colored ones. I asked, "Where are all the other colors of flowers?"

#4. I was trying to select a summer top and the only two-piece ensembles which appeared on the pages were violet-colored.

This is a very rare instance in which The Holy Spirit confirmed in real-time what He'd shown me in the Spirit. Since my husband and I had served on the governmental mountain for over three decades, I was quite surprised at my new assignment.

An Invitation

There's a clarion call being issued to the intercessors, "Cast off your discouragement but not your confidence, dig out your needles, and resume knitting (praying)."

Some of you will be issued more than one color of yarn as you will be assigned to more than one mountain.

God will confirm these colors and prayer assignments to you in several ways, one of which will be that you will start to repeatedly encounter the color through various, unexpected means.

After praying through this prophetic vision and message, what colors has God assigned to you, and how have you implemented them?

_____
_____
_____
_____

Any of you who knit in real life, I would welcome your input after reading this blog post.

This prophetic word is for both women and men. God, the "Master Knitter," is connecting the hearts of believers to supernaturally transform His 7 mountains of culture. I've never learned how to knit, but He's teaching me how to effectively pray through the power of The Holy Spirit for this specific assignment. Will you please join me? _____

Sheila Eismann, Prophetic Seer, Blogger, Author & Teacher, publishes her weekly blog posts endeavoring to encourage others through God's word. Her writings include teaching and instructions on how to apply prophetic insights for daily living. Please subscribe to receive new blog posts on her website at www.sheilaeismann.com. by clicking the "Subscribe" button in the far upper right-hand corner of her Home webpage.

Double Divine Justice ~ The Blindfolds Are Suddenly Removed!

April 21, 2021
Prophetic Visions

As a child, do you remember playing the game "Pin The Tail On The Donkey?" During my grade school years and when attending some birthday parties, this was one of the faves. This week's prophetic blog post addresses the subject of double divine justice wherein the blindfolds are suddenly removed to enable clear vision.

This blog post is Part VII in my "Prophetic Personal Growth Series" which is based upon a shift in the prophetic words, dreams, and visions that I've been given from the Lord which is geared more toward the individual as opposed to countries, cities, entities, and so forth.

In a recent prophetic vision, I saw a woman standing by herself in a spacious, outdoor setting. She'd been groping around in the darkness trying to find her way. **Suddenly**, her blindfold was removed! This eye covering looked more like a rectangular-shaped, cotton, white dishtowel that had been tied around her eyes similar to what would be used in the child's game referenced in the above paragraph.

The strange thing is after it was supernaturally removed, the woman finally came to the realization it had been impeding her vision the entire time. Granted, had she been aware of the blindfold, she could have reached behind her head and untied it, but this was not the case.

The accompanying image is the closest one I could find to convey the prophetic message even though this woman is not standing in a spacious setting.

The Healing Tower

In the next scene of this vision, the woman appeared at the top of a high tower. She was watching a movie. Various, challenging scenes from her life began to appear on the screen. At the end of each episode, rather than the typical credits listed for producer, director, screen play, costume design, musical score, etc., these words appeared, "The following explains why this event happened the way it did: _____

_____."

I heard the sound of a key unlocking a door inside of her. The past was obviously behind her now as a broad vista of understanding opened unto her to usher in a profound, quick spiritual, emotional, and mental healing.

The woman's mind traveled back in time throughout her life. She started having all of these "aha moments" wherein she would exclaim, "Oh, I can see clearly now! That's why thus and such turned out the way that it did."

She can now fully embrace Romans 8:28, "And we know that all things work together for good to those who love God, to those who are the called according to *His* purpose."

Waves of Refreshing and Revelation

In the last scene of the vision, the woman was relaxing in a quiet alcove of water near a beach which is symbolic of safety, boundaries, battlegrounds, limits, and recreation. Rays of sunlight glistened through her long, copper-colored hair. Copper is representative of strength, righteousness, and boldness. Ministering angels dried her tears. Gentle waves of refreshing and revelation washed over her and lapped onto the white, fine-sand shore. She proclaimed, "My life will never be the same again!"

This woman clearly understood she couldn't change the past injustices in her life, but she could now shift into high gear to receive her healing, recompense, and restoration.

While this prophetic vision has more of a spiritual emphasis (2 Corinthians 3:12-16), I heard God announce in the Spirit, "I am healing conditions pertaining to sight, both spiritually and physically."

Pay Attention to The Suddenly Moments In Your Life

The ***suddenly*** aspect of this vision reminded me of the Apostle Paul and his encounter with Jesus on the Road to Damascus in Acts 9:1-9.
"Then Saul, still breathing threats and murder against the disciples of the Lord, went to the high priest and asked letters from him to the synagogues of Damascus, so that if he found any who were of the Way, whether men or women, he might bring them bound to Jerusalem.

As he journeyed he came near Damascus, and **suddenly** a light shone around him from heaven. Then he fell to the ground, and heard a voice saying to him, 'Saul, Saul, why are you persecuting Me?' (Emphasis mine) And he said, 'Who are You, Lord?'

Then the Lord said, 'I am Jesus, whom you are persecuting. It *is* hard for you to kick against the goads.'

So he, trembling and astonished, said, 'Lord, what do You want me to do?'

Then the Lord *said* to him, 'Arise and go into the city, and you will be told what you must do.'

And the men who journeyed with him stood speechless, hearing a voice but seeing no one. Then Saul arose from the ground, and when his eyes were opened he saw no one. But they led him by the hand and brought *him* into Damascus. And he was three days without sight, and neither ate nor drank." As we continue reading through this passage of scripture, we see where Ananias laid his hands on Saul. Acts 9:18 reads, "Immediately there fell from his eyes *something* like scales, and he received his sight at once; and he arose and was baptized."

If you study the remainder of the book of Acts along with several other books of the New Testament, you will indeed discover that Paul's life was never the same once he could see clearly and discern the path for his life. All of us are beneficiaries of this as he penned two-thirds of the New Testament.

Since God is no respecter of persons, He can orchestrate a divine suddenly for you just like He did for His servant, The Apostle Paul. Purpose to watch for yours as it will be life-changing irrespective of your current age.

https://sheilaeismann.com/the-parable-of-the-talents/

Double Divine Justice

The following was impressed upon my spirit: There's a double divine justice coming which is the recompense of justice for the one who has been blindfolded and a meting out of justice for the one who placed the blindfold upon the other person if he or she does not repent.

The Greek word for recompense is *antapodidomi* which in a good sense means to repay or requite. (Luke 14:14; Romans 11:35: and 1 Thessalonians 3:9) The unfavorable aspect of this word is penalty and vengeance.

https://www.blueletterbible.org/lang/Lexicon/Lexicon.cfm?strongs=G467&t=KJV

Prophetic Insights For Daily Living

#1. There will be a circumstance or situation in which you'll suddenly recognize this blindfold has been placed upon you just before it is supernaturally removed. It will be a major turning point in your life. This will be an epiphany or "aha" moment where **suddenly,** you'll be able to see clearly, and things will change for the better forever in a moment's time.

#2. Once this happens, it's paramount you extend 100% forgiveness to the person(s) who placed the blindfold upon you even if he or she has passed away or you can no longer locate or contact him or her.

#3. As you travel back in time, you'll be able to see how this blindfold has affected every sphere of your life, but most importantly, your decisions. It's very difficult to make wise choices when we don't have clear vision. Please make some notations here if you desire to do so:

_____
_____
_____
_____

#4. God is in the recompense and restoration business. No one does it better in His kingdom or His economy. Trust God to bring these to you, so you can devote your time and energy to fulfilling your God-given destiny. Praise, worship, and honor Him for His divine, orchestrated acts of recompense and restoration, so you can have clear vision moving forward. Has God moved on your behalf regarding recompense and restoration?

_____
_____
_____
_____

#5. Beloved, may we accept and appropriate the deep, inner workings in our life by God Who is the Maker of our life. As we walk with Him, His Son, Jesus, and The Holy Spirit, we're completing every page of our books that have already been written in heaven. (Daniel 7:10; Psalm 139:16; 1 Corinthians 13:11-15; and Ephesians 1:11, 2:10, and 4:1)

#6. Pray and ask God to redeem the time you've lost due to being blindfolded. Do you need to have any time redeemed?

_____
_____
_____
_____

#7. While this prophetic blog post deals with a temporary blindness, we must always have compassion upon those with sight challenges.

Fellow brothers and sisters, may we all trust Jesus to bring justice to victory in the necessary areas of our lives. (Matthew 12:20) Meanwhile, let us continue to trust Him as He is the blessed controller of ALL things.

Sheila Eismann, Prophetic Seer, Blogger, Author & Teacher, publishes her weekly blog posts endeavoring to encourage others through God's word. Her writings include teaching and instructions on how to apply prophetic insights for daily living. Please subscribe to receive new blog posts on her website at www.sheilaeismann.com. by clicking the "Subscribe" button in the far upper right-hand corner of her Home webpage.

Sheila Eismann

Beneficial Boundaries

April 29, 2021
Prophetic Visions

This is Part VIII in my "Prophetic Personal Growth Series" which is based upon a shift in the prophetic words, dreams, and visions that I've been given from the Lord of late which are geared more toward the individual as opposed to countries, cities, entities, and so forth. This particular one addresses the need for beneficial boundaries as a result of a broken fence.

On Friday morning, April 23, 2021, I was taken into a vision in a rural setting. This particular residence was blessed with a large, spacious yard. Even though the house was in the country rather than the suburbs, there was an old, weathered fence that surrounded the property. It was in a real state of disrepair as some of the boards were broken and falling down. Black mold was beginning to grow on others.

When the Holy Spirit zoomed in closer, I saw a snake slithering through one of the areas of the broken fence.

In contrasting wisdom versus folly in the book of Ecclesiastes, King Solomon stated,

"He who digs a pit will fall into it,

And whoever breaks through a wall will be bitten by a serpent." (Ecclesiastes 10:8)

In this verse, one piece of the king's advice is that people are not to meddle or intrude where they do not belong, especially in the life of another. Snakes sometimes like to hide in hedges or near piles of wood. In Acts 28:3, Luke tells us all about the Apostle Paul's experience with a viper hidden in a bundle of sticks.

The symbolisms for snakes need no real explanation; however, some of them are: sin, the tempter, the devil, false teachers, a lying spirit, curse, hypocrisy, curses, seduction, fear, witchcraft, and division. This is by no means an exhaustive list.

The Greek word for bound (noun form) is *horothesia* (Strongs G3734), which is the fixing of a boundary rather than the boundary itself (from horos, a boundary, and *tithemi*, to place), which is used in Acts 17:26, *bounds*.

https://www.blueletterbible.org/lang/lexicon/lexicon.cfm?Strongs=G3734&t=KJV

Perhaps another way to envision this exercise would be to use the term "limit-placing." It's important to understand that the onus is on each individual to set his or her own limits according to Biblical standards and not those of the secular world.

When authoring my women's Bible study titled *A Woman of Substance*, I delve into this subject in greater detail in Chapter 7 thereof.

The Third Watch Of The Night

As the second scene of this prophetic vision unfolded, I saw a woman walking around the inside of the perimeter of her fence. She seemed somewhat irritated and surprised at the condition of the same. Sitting inside her house and stewing about it until the wee hours of the morning, she donned her head lamp, grabbed a flashlight, and headed outside. This was during the 3rd watch of the night which is between midnight and 3:00 a.m. when evil and its deeds rise to their zenith. It was not revealed to me what she found during her search.

Angelic Help Is On The Way

Angels appeared in the last scene of this vision who are assigned to the repair project. Instead of sashes around their waists, they wore leather tool belts that contained a hammer, nails, measuring tape, and assorted other small tools. A load of new, fresh cedar boards had been delivered in the driveway of the owner's home. Branded into the new boards was the word **WISDOM.**

https://sheilaeismann.com/heart-of-wisdom/

Since there have already been several excellent books written about boundaries and the importance of how they relate to our Christian lives, it's not my intent to reinvent the wheel in this week's blog post.

Prophetic Insights For Daily Living:

1. The Bible is written for our instruction (Romans 15:4), so can you think of someone mentioned therein who did not bother to establish boundaries in his or her life and the disastrous consequences as a result thereof?

2. What is likely to happen in our lives if we do not set Godly limits or boundaries?

3. If you are presently in that situation, what new limits need to be established or boundary lines drawn to bring about the freedom that you have in Jesus Christ? (John 8:32, 2 Corinthians 3:17, and Galatians 5:1)

4. In this vision, the old, weathered, and molded boards represent old boundaries that need to be replaced.

5. Assess your fence/boundaries. Take a look at it through a new set of spiritual lenses. What does it look like? Even if you don't live in an area with a literal fence, this prophetic vision could still apply to you or someone you know.

_____

_____

_____

_____

The Lord Jesus is always so faithful to bring to our attention the repairs and adjustments that need to be made in our lives. While it may not always seem pleasant or necessary, we can always trust Him as He has our best interest at heart.

"Thus says the Lord, your Redeemer,
The Holy One of Israel:
"I *am* the Lord your God,
Who teaches you to profit,
Who leads you by the way you should go." (Isaiah 48:17)

Sheila Eismann, Prophetic Seer, Blogger, Author & Teacher, publishes her weekly blog posts endeavoring to encourage others through God's word. Her writings include teaching and instructions on how to apply prophetic insights for daily living. Please subscribe to receive new blog posts on her website at www.sheilaeismann.com. by clicking the "Subscribe" button in the far upper right-hand corner of her Home webpage.

Strength, Dignity & Laughter In Our Immediate Future

May 5, 2021
Prophetic Teachings

The last 21 verses of the final chapter of Proverbs in the Bible have some very sage advice. Even though they pertain to the epilogue of the wife of noble character, verse 25 could apply to both men and women, "She is clothed with strength and dignity; she can laugh at the days to come." (NIV) In the past couple of weeks, The Holy Spirit has impressed upon me the importance of evaluating our physical and spiritual clothing as it's all about strength, dignity, & laughter in our immediate future. 'Tis time for a wardrobe check!

The Hebrew word for strength in Proverbs 31:25 is **oz** (Strong's H5797).

https://www.blueletterbible.org/lang/Lexicon/Lexicon.cfm?page=2&strongs=H5797&t=KJV#lexResults

There are various applications for this word which are force, security, majesty, praise, boldness, loudness, might, power, strength, and strong.

Lebus (Strong's H3830) is the Hebrew word for clothing in Proverbs 31:25 which includes a garment (literally or figuratively), apparel, clothed with, garment, raiment, vestment, and vesture.

https://www.blueletterbible.org/lang/Lexicon/Lexicon.cfm?strongs=H3830&t=KJV

Body Armor Adds Strength

Our correct wardrobe will serve as a form of body armor to assist with laughter in our immediate future. While other verses in Proverbs Chapter 31 address the noble wife's business acumen and other characteristics, verse 25 speaks of her **material, physical, personal, social, and political strength** based upon the explanation of the Strong's definition. These garments are worn in conjunction with her dignity and honor. She's worthy of honor and respect which denotes a sense of pride in oneself coupled with self-respect.

Let's look at each of these aspects of strength to help each of us determine where we need assistance. It's sort of like looking through your wardrobe or clothes closet to evaluate if you need to get rid of some old items, keep some existing ones, or acquire new apparel.

#1. Material

#2. Physical

#3. Personal

#4. Social

#5. Political

For a practical application, let's select #4 above which is "social." In light of all that's going on in our country right now, it's imperative that we literally and figuratively take stock of what we're wearing at all times.

I would encourage you to spend some quality, quiet time with Jesus and allow Him to speak to you by and through His Word and the power of His Holy Spirit regarding this subject matter.

Record what He shows you and act upon it accordingly. This is a great exercise to add to your prophetic journaling. If you've not yet implemented it, I would highly suggest it as it's a great faith builder to look back and see how God is working in your life and calculate your spiritual growth in Him.

_____
_____
_____
_____
_____

Put On The Lord Jesus Christ

In Romans 13:14, The Apostle Paul instructs Christians, "But put on the Lord Jesus Christ, and make no provision for the flesh, to *fulfill* its lusts."

The wording *put on Christ* means to figuratively clothe oneself with the Lord Jesus Christ, so we can reveal God's glory to the world through His one and only begotten Son.

Paul is speaking of donning spiritual clothing because when we do this, we don't focus on gratifying the desires of the sinful nature which every person is born with. (Romans 5:12) The "old clothing" in our closet refers to the sinful nature and habits we're still wearing and walking in, if applicable.

We must purpose to dress in the appropriate outfit for each new day. Here are some verses to assist in this regard:

Romans 3:22, 8:29 and 12:2
1 Corinthians 1:30
2 Corinthians 5:21
Galatians 3:27
Ephesians 4:24; 6:11-18
Colossians 3:10, 12

What additional verses or concepts could you add to this list?

_____
_____
_____
_____

Borrowed &/Or Appropriate Clothing

As the Holy Spirit has been helping me write this message, He stressed the importance of wearing one's own clothing. Granted, this has more of a spiritual application for this message than a physical one.

In prior decades, it was a very common practice to borrow physical clothing from someone which continues present day. I especially think of wedding dresses in this regard since that can be one of the main expenses for a bride's special day.

Fast forward to the Parable of the Wedding Feast in Matthew 22:1-14.

"And Jesus answered and spoke to them again by parables and said: 'The kingdom of heaven is like a certain king who arranged a marriage for his son, and sent out his servants to call those who were invited to the wedding; and they were not willing to come. Again, he sent out other servants, saying, 'Tell those who are invited, 'See, I have prepared my dinner; my oxen and fatted cattle *are* killed, and all things *are* ready. Come to the wedding.' But they made light of it and went their ways, one to his own farm, another to his business. And the rest seized his servants, treated *them* spitefully, and killed *them*. But when the king heard *about it,* he was furious. And he sent out his armies, destroyed those murderers, and burned up their city. Then he said to his servants, 'The wedding is ready, but those who were invited were not worthy. Therefore go into the highways, and as many as you find, invite to the wedding.' So those servants went out into the highways and gathered together all whom they found, both bad and good. And the wedding *hall* was filled with guests. "But when the king came in to see the guests, he saw a man there who did not have on a wedding garment. So he said to him, 'Friend, how did you come in here without a wedding garment?' And he was speechless. Then the king said to the servants, 'Bind him hand and foot, take him away, and cast *him* into outer darkness; there will be weeping and gnashing of teeth.' "For many are called, but few *are* chosen."

As you read through the above passage of scripture, what is The Holy Spirit speaking to you or impressing upon your spirit regarding a wardrobe check?

_____
_____
_____
_____

Prophetic Insights For Daily Living

1. Putting on the Lord Jesus Christ means to continually abide in Him. (John 15:4-10)

2. If we're clothed with Jesus, we exhibit all of the characteristics, graces, and qualities which are in Him.

3. Jesus must not only be our Savior but our Lord as well. This is known as "Lordship Salvation." Otherwise, it would be like wearing a half and half garment which is one part Godly and the other portion worldly.

4. When we become a disciple of Jesus Christ, our lives become conformed to His image, so we become that living epistle for the rest of the world to read. Envision yourself being invited to give a speech on the world's stage. What would you choose to wear? Would you perform a wardrobe check before walking onto the platform? (2 Corinthians 3:2-3)

_____
_____

When we're clothed with strength and dignity via our Lord Jesus Christ, this affords us the opportunity for laughter in our immediate future. Inherent within this laughter is confidence, dignity, rejoicing, self-confidence, security, strength, Godly power, and boldness.

As for me, I desire to be able to laugh at the days to come! A merry heart doeth good like a medicine. Godly joy and laughter are formidable weapons we can implement during times of spiritual warfare.

https://sheilaeismann.com/fill-your-cup-with-joy/

Having a joyful, happy heart is good medicine and a cheerful mind can help with spiritual and physical healing. After completing your wardrobe check, make sure to take a look in the mirror as one of the most important things we wear every day is our smile!

Sheila Eismann, Prophetic Seer, Blogger, Author & Teacher, publishes her weekly blog posts endeavoring to encourage others through God's word. Her writings include teaching and instructions on how to apply prophetic insights for daily living. Please subscribe to receive new blog posts on her website at www.sheilaeismann.com. by clicking the "Subscribe" button in the far upper right-hand corner of her Home webpage.

Sheila Eismann

The Seed Bag, The New Field & The Scarecrow

May 12, 2021
Prophetic Visions

Springtime in our area finds farmers, ranchers, and some gardeners working from sunrise to sunset. After preparing the soil, they carefully select the types of seeds to plant. The prophetic message I've been receiving over the past few days includes the seed bag, the new field, and the scarecrow which can seem like a fairly predictable combination. God can and does oftentimes use the cycles of nature and everyday things in our lives to impart spiritual lessons and messages to us. This is the time to plan your harvest.

Scene #1 of prophetic vision:

When the vision opened, I saw a man dressed in farmer's clothing sitting at a table. There was a large burlap bag of seeds placed on the floor to the right side of him. He would reach inside the bag, grab a fistful of the seeds, and spread them on the table. He adjusted his reading glasses as he examined each seed very closely. The name of the seed appeared on each one.

As I watched this scene unfold, it reminded me of my dad who used to sit at our kitchen table inside our house on Sage Creek Farms and sort dried beans, so my sweet mother could make navy bean and ham soup. Since the beans were field run, it was important to sort them ahead of time to make sure the small gravel and other debris didn't end up in the soup and break a tooth!

Scene #2 of prophetic vision:

In the next scene, the Spirit opened up, and I saw an expansive, agricultural field that had been recently plowed, disked, harrowed, and readied for immediate planting.

It's important to note that nothing had been grown in this field before. It's farm land at its very best.

Scene #3 of prophetic vision:

The scarecrow appeared in the last scene of this ongoing vision which serves as a decoy in human form. It's usually dressed in ragged clothing along with a straw hat and set in open fields. While it's supposed to keep crows and other bandits from stealing freshly planted seeds and disturbing the newly tilled soil, the method is highly ineffective. Since it's a delicate time frame before each seed sprouts, the area must be protected.

Crows are intelligent birds, and they realize in short order that the figure in the field is just a dummy or decoy. 'Tis not too long before they're back to their old tactics which are to steal, kill, and destroy crops.

Just as today's farmers and ranchers have had to resort to new methods to preserve their crops by applying potent, smelly objects or organic sprays and building fences to keep some wildlife out, we're living in a day and age when we need to rely upon The Holy Spirit to help us wage daily warfare to keep the thief and predators out of our lives.

Your Field In Full Bloom

Since one of the symbolisms for a field is a Christian believer, we must be intentional in our planting. The non-believers, naysayers, critics, blasphemers, and all sorts of other folks are watching what will bloom in our fields.

The long game is our harvest. All of us are writing our epistles from the time we plant our first seed until it's in full bloom.

"You are our epistle written in our hearts, known and read by all men; clearly *you are* an epistle of Christ, ministered by us, written not with ink but by the Spirit of the living God, not on tablets of stone but on tablets of flesh, *that is,* of the heart." (2 Corinthians 3:2-3)

Some crops will have varying yields in different seasons in our lives, but the emphasis of this prophetic message is upon selecting correct seeds before planting them.

https://sheilaeismann.com/spiritual-time/

Loosestrife Can Be A Pervasive Problem:

Lining the ditch banks and sprinkled across some pastures and fields in our geographic region is a beautiful purple plant named "strife." While it's pleasant to the eyes, purple loosestrife negatively affects both wildlife and agriculture. It displaces and replaces native flora and fauna, eliminating food, nesting, and shelter for wildlife. By reducing habitat size, purple loosestrife harms fish spawning and waterfowl habitat.

It is a vigorous competitor and can crowd out other vegetation including native species. In addition, it can quickly dominate a site and adapt to environmental changes. Loosestrife stands provide poor cover for waterfowl.

This is a noxious weed that is extremely difficult to get rid of and can overtake an area in a very short period of time.

https://www.nwcb.wa.gov/weeds/purple-loosestrife

The spiritual analogy is that once our field is planted, we must be vigilant to protect it from noxious weeds and anything that would overtake it negatively.

The law of sowing and reaping is always applicable. We do indeed reap what we sow. (Hosea 8:7, 10:12; 2 Corinthians 9:6-11; and Galatians 6:7-9)

Prophetic Insights For Daily Living

#1. Stand on the promise of seedtime and harvest.

"While the earth remains, seedtime and harvest, cold and heat, winter and summer, and day and night shall not cease." (Genesis 8:22)

There are over 50 seedtime and harvest scriptures in the Bible. If you are someone who enjoys topical studies, this is a great suggestion for you along with prophetic journaling.

_____
_____

_____

_____

#2. Take stock or inventory of what you're planting right now. It's a new season, and you're being given fresh seeds to plant in a new field.

_____

_____

_____

_____

<u>What's in your seed bag?</u>

Our daily actions and choices are analogous to sowing seeds that take root in other people's lives and produce a harvest.

An example of this would be a family we know in real life who has a small farm a few miles southwest of us. Every member of this family is as reliable as the sun rising every morning. If someone needs something, especially during a dire emergency, these people are always at the ready and know exactly what practical things to do.

Another illustration would be the compassionate folks who minister to those who are undergoing severe trials, tribulations, and health challenges. Their mercy anointing freely flows which is such a gift in and of itself.

#3. It's all about the future harvest fields in your life.

Where are you planting your seeds?

Family

Church

Work

Neighborhood

School

Geographic Region

In what other fields are you currently planted or have you been assigned? If you're unsure, pray and God will definitely lead you in the right direction and reveal this to you. He's looking for a willing heart and spirit, flexibility, faithfulness, and you say "Yes" when He asks and directs you.

#4. What kind of harvest do you desire to produce?

When your field is in full bloom, what will it look like? Will it be pleasant to view along with releasing a sweet aroma? We are the fragrance of Christ everywhere we go. (2 Corinthians 2:15-17)

_____
_____
_____
_____

#5. Are there effective weapons of warfare that you need to implement or increase to replace the ineffective "scarecrow" in your field to ensure a bountiful harvest? Also, do you need to guard against loosestrife encroaching into your new field?

_____
_____
_____
_____

Some of our spiritual weapons include:

The word of God – Hebrews 4:12

Prayer – 2 Corinthians 3-6; James 5:16-18

Fasting – Ezra 8:21-23; Matthew 17:20-21

Praise and worship – Psalm 100:4, 138:1-3

Praying in the Spirit – 1 Corinthians 14:2, 14-15; Romans 8:26; Jude 20

Obedience to Christ – 1 Samuel 15:22-23; John 14:21, 23-24

Putting on the armor of God – Ephesians 6:10-18

The name of Jesus – John 16:23-24, 26-27

Pleading the blood of Jesus – Revelation 12:10

Our Christian testimony – Revelation 12:10

Our faith in Jesus – 1 John 5:4

Dwelling in unity with other Christian believers helps to afford strength and protection for all of us – Psalm 133; 1 Corinthians 1:10 and Ephesians 4:5-6

Are there other weapons of warfare you would like to add to this list or additional scriptures to accompany the aforementioned?

_____
_____
_____
_____

We appropriate prophetic messages by faith as we pray into them, act upon the directives inherent therein, and trust God, Jesus, and The Holy Spirit to implement them in our lives. They are ever-present and ready to help us plan our harvest. I would like to close this week's blog post with The Apostle Paul's prayer for the church at Philippi,

"Not that I seek the gift, but I seek the fruit that abounds to your account. Indeed I have all and abound. I am full, having received from Epaphroditus the things *sent* from you, a sweet-smelling aroma, an acceptable sacrifice, well-pleasing to God. And my God shall supply all your need according to His riches in glory by Christ Jesus." (Philippians 4:17-19)

Sheila Eismann, Prophetic Seer, Blogger, Author & Teacher, publishes her weekly blog posts endeavoring to encourage others through God's word. Her writings include teaching and instructions on how to apply prophetic insights for daily living. Please subscribe to receive new blog posts on her website at www.sheilaeismann.com. by clicking the "Subscribe" button in the far upper right-hand corner of her Home webpage.

Ride & Decree Victory!

May 19, 2021
Prophetic Words

Would you enjoy a hot air balloon ride? If so, now is your appointed hour. You have the golden opportunity to take a trip, not powered by the normal burner fueled by propane as is customarily used for a hot air balloon, but by the might and power of The Holy Spirit of God. It's time to take a ride and decree victory. Pentecost ushered in the days of jubilant triumph!

Up, Up, and Away!

On Pentecost Eve, May 16, 2021, the Spirit realm opened, and I saw a young woman riding in a hot air balloon. She appeared to be in her mid to late '30s. Blonde-haired angels, wearing white robes with navy blue sashes, were standing on each side of her. Navy (dark) blue represents authority and The Holy Spirit.

One of the angels gave the woman a gold signet ring. A scroll was handed to her by another angel. There were instructions affixed to the outside of the scroll which read,

"UPON OPENING THIS SCROLL, PROPHESY AND DECREE WHAT IS WRITTEN INSIDE."

A hot air balloon symbolizes ministry in the Spirit and being transported in the Spirit. Corresponding scriptures are as follows:

"So the Spirit lifted me up and took me away, and I went in bitterness, in the heat of my spirit; but the hand of the Lord was strong upon me." (Ezekiel 3:14)

"He stretched out the form of a hand, and took me by a lock of my hair; and the Spirit lifted me up between earth and heaven, and brought me in visions of God to Jerusalem, to the door of the north gate of the inner *court,* where the seat of the image of jealousy *was,* which provokes to jealousy." (Ezekiel 8:3)

"Then the Spirit lifted me up and brought me to the East Gate of the Lord's house, which faces eastward; and there at the door of the gate were twenty-five men, among whom I saw Jaazaniah the son of Azzur, and Pelatiah the son of Benaiah, princes of the people." (Ezekiel 11:1)

"Now when they came up out of the water, the Spirit of the Lord caught Philip away, so that the eunuch saw him no more; and he went on his way rejoicing." (Acts 8:39)

For further information as to how hot air balloons actually function, here's a link:

https://www.google.com/search?q=how+does+a+hot+air+balloon+work&oq=how+does+a+hot+air+balloon+work&aqs=chrome..69i57j0l9.4272j0j7&sourceid=chrome&ie=UTF-8

True Magnetic North

When I first saw the hot air balloon, it was carrying the woman in a westward direction and then veered to the north. I saw boundary lines that were formed by solid, neon, medium blue colored lines. Just inside those lines was another one which appeared as neon yellow. Even though it was broad daylight, these boundary lines were very evident and defined. The hot air balloon stayed within the boundary lines as it floated in the air.

West(ward) symbolizes departure from God or God departing; a setting down or an end. The important thing is that the Spirit quickly and supernaturally directed the balloon in a north(ward) direction which indicates the place of God's throne, location of the enemy, or moving into your spiritual inheritance.

Just as the woman in the hot air balloon was surrounded by heavenly angels, we have angels assigned to us. Everyone has their own personal angels as evidenced by Matthew 18:10 and Acts 12:5-15.

What was impressed upon my spirit was that we're to be riding with and staying very close to our Lord Jesus Christ as directed by The Holy Spirit. He's the wind/power that should be operating in our life.

We are living in the days when we must come up higher (get in the hot air balloon) and travel with The Holy Spirit, go where He wants to take us, and not rely on our own understanding which is unprofitable.

Proverbs 3:5-6 carries the following instructions,

"Trust in the Lord with all your heart,
And lean not on your own understanding;
In all your ways acknowledge Him,
And He shall direct your paths."

Take Your Seat At The Heavenly Table With Christ Jesus

Things look very different from an aerial, spiritual view as opposed to ground level. To triumph, we need to know what's actually going on in our personal lives, our nation, and our world.

The hallmark scripture to accompany our hot air balloon ride is Ephesians 2:4-7 which reads,

"But God, who is rich in mercy, because of His great love with which He loved us, even when we were dead in trespasses, made us alive together with Christ (by grace you have been saved), and raised *us* up together, and made *us* sit together in the heavenly *places* in Christ Jesus, that in the ages to come He might show the exceeding riches of His grace in *His* kindness toward us in Christ Jesus."

Prophetic Insights For Daily Living

1, What's written on the scroll are the present-day declarations and adjustments for our lives to help us function amid everything that's going on.
2. This is not a one-size-fits-all as the scroll is unique and tailor-made for each one of us. It's a throne room issued a decree which carries much weight and spiritual authority.
3. These are positive declarations that pertain to the direction of your life. They are not negative declarations or pronouncements of judgments.
4. What I was shown in The Spirit regarding the woman in the balloon was the following, **"I am no longer under the thumb of _____**

(whoever this other person was). John 8:36." She prophesied and decreed what was written in her scroll.

5. As odd as it may sound, perhaps the woman riding in the hot air balloon didn't fully realize she was in this condition until she was taken high in the spiritual realm where's she's seated in the heavenly places with Christ Jesus. The goal is to set this woman free, so she can become all that God has destined for her to be and fulfill her books of destiny. (Daniel 7:10; Psalm 139:16; and Ephesians 1:11, 2:10 and 4:1)

6. Some of the decrees written inside your scroll will be victories for the biggest battles you're in right now.

_____
_____
_____
_____

7. There are corresponding scriptures that accompany each of the prophetic decrees and declarations. You will be shown these as you partner with The Holy Spirit in this spiritual exercise.

_____
_____
_____
_____

8. An example of a prophetic declaration can be found in Matthew 16:15-19, "He [Jesus] said to them, 'But who do you say that I am?' Simon Peter answered and said, 'You are the Christ, the Son of the living God. 'Jesus answered and said to him, 'Blessed are you, Simon Bar-Jonah, for flesh and blood has not revealed *this* to you, but My Father who is in heaven. And I also say to you that you are Peter, and on this rock I will build My church, and the

gates of Hades shall not prevail against it. And I will give you the keys of the kingdom of heaven, and whatever you bind on earth will be bound in heaven, and whatever you loose on earth will be loosed in heaven.'"

9. Death and life are in the power of the tongue. (Proverbs 18:21) Our words carry positive and negative weight in the spiritual atmospheres and realms. Can you think of a time when this has applied to your life or has your life been affected in some manner by someone else's words?

_____
_____
_____
_____

10. We're either justified or condemned by our words. (Matthew 12:37)

Beneficial Boundaries

One of my recent blog posts dealt with establishing beneficial boundaries which would be a helpful companion read along with this week's prophetic message.

https://sheilaeismann.com/broken-fence/

Upon receiving this prophetic, revelatory download about the hot air balloon ride, I felt directed by The Holy Spirit to take a prayer walk on Pentecost, May 17, 2021, since 17 is symbolic of victory.

The Holy Spirit directed my victorious, prophetic utterances as I walked the route He planned for me. In real life, I don't own a gold, signet ring such as was given to the woman in the hot air balloon.

In Old Testament times, after kings signed their decrees, they would seal them with their signet rings which represent identity, seal, authority, and position. Believers in Jesus are kings and priests under the New Covenant. (1 Peter 2:9 and Revelation 1:6) In my mind's eye, I can affix the seal of the signet ring to each of my prophetic decrees after pronouncing them.

The release of heavenly, spiritual revelation is just one of the **key aspects** surrounding the time frame of Pentecost. My heartfelt prayer is that you will decide to take your ride, decree victory, and triumph in every area of your life!

God has blessed each of us with the supreme ability to achieve our goals, the courage to pursue our dreams, and the faith to believe in His promises.

Sheila Eismann, Prophetic Seer, Blogger, Author & Teacher, publishes her weekly blog posts endeavoring to encourage others through God's word. Her writings include teaching and instructions on how to apply prophetic insights for daily living. Please subscribe to receive new blog posts on her website at www.sheilaeismann.com. by clicking the "Subscribe" button in the far upper right-hand corner of her Home webpage.

Sheila Eismann, Idaho native, author, and publisher of 15 books was raised on Sage Creek Farms in Southwestern Idaho. She pens inspirational and fictional books drawing upon her life experiences as a legal secretary, law firm office administrator, office manager for a national horse breed registry, and successful operator of a bookkeeping business. Midway through life, she discovered published authors and poets on both sides of her family. Eismann, a co-founder of ICAN (Idaho Creative Author's Network), speaks at Writer's and Women's Conferences. She endeavors to be an encourager with a sense of humor. Learn more about Sheila, read her weekly blog posts, and discover her books at **www.sheilaeismann.com.**

Where to find Sheila Eismann online:

Email: sheila@sheilaeismann.com

Website: www.sheilaeismann.com

Facebook: www.facebook.com/sheila.eismann

Blog: www.sheilaeismann.com

LinkedIn: Sheila Eismann

Sheila's and Dan's books are also featured online in Sheila's Etsy shop: www.etsy.com/shop/BooksbySheilaEismann

Sheila invites you to check out her new website **www.sheilaeismann.com** and sign up to receive her blog posts in your email inbox. Please send her an email at **sheila@sheilaeismann.com** to say hello and to let her know what ministered to you the most in this workbook or your favorite blog post. Happy reading and studying!

OTHER BOOKS AVAILABLE FROM AUTHORS SHEILA EISMANN, DAN EISMANN & DESERT SAGE PRESS which can be purchased from: www.sheilaeismann.com **or** www.amazon.com.

Read and study with **Sheila Eismann,** Prophetic Author, Blogger, Speaker and Teacher, in Volume 1 of her latest series titled ***Prophetic Insights for Daily Living.*** This **231-page** workbook can be used as a stand-alone devotional, individual Bible Study or in a group study. Sheila describes various dreams, visions, prophetic words and teachings she's been given by The Holy Spirit from August 2020 through December 2020 which are designed to help you grow in spiritual knowledge and the operation of The Holy Spirit gifts. Each entry includes either questions, contemplation, reflection, or a call to action.

Western Fiction Book One of The Sabblonti Series, ***Jantzi's Jokers***, features Jantzi Belle, the matriarch of the Sabblonti family, who has worked for decades to keep her cattle empire intact. Life takes a drastic turn when she receives a late-night visitor. The brief disappearance of her Last Will and Testament could complicate matters between her daughters, Stormy and Sarita. Stormy and her husband, Chet Castins, are struggling to work through the loss of their three children. Against all odds, drifter Wyn Moreland makes a bold move when he decides that Sarita is his beauty to rescue. The county veterinarian, Dr. Ben Shaw, is also vying for her affections. Will Wyn emerge as the winner? Just before the dawn of the New Year, revelations come forth regarding forgery, cattle rustling, and land exploitation. Will the Sabblonti Empire survive, and more importantly, who will control its reins?

The Sabblonti Saga accelerates in Book Two of the Series, **A Stormy Year**. Riding her high horse after inheriting the family fortune, Stormy Castins is determined to reinvent herself following her husband's accident. Blinded by jealousy, ambition, and naivety, she hires Less and Meg Alotto to oversee her vast high desert mountain domain. While Stormy is away, the cattle herd ends up in disarray.

Amidst the hot dry season, romance is blooming on several fronts despite a major showdown during a mid-summer celebration. The pesky Black Raven continues to wreak havoc at the most inopportune times.

Unable to overcome the vengeance which strikes by way of a mysterious range fire combined with the dire deeds of a cagey couple, the Sabblonti Ranch is in shambles just as Stormy starts to regain her senses. Humility is the prescription needed to open her eyes in order to realize what's truly important in life. The sparks from a belated holiday rendevous set Chet and Stormy on their path to recovery.

Desperation explodes when heiress Stormy Sabblonti Castins calculates her dwindling fortune in Book 3 of the Sabblonti Series, **Love the Tie that Binds.** Is she capable of learning the painful lessons of having to rely upon someone and something other than inherited wealth? As her husband, Chet, continues to heal from his near fatal accident, tormenting shadows of The Black Raven lurk in the background.

These high desert hills are alive with blessed babies, enchanting engagements, skillful scavengers, sophisticated scoundrels, rich revelations, timeless treasures, and western weddings.

The Main Sabblonti Ranch house abounds with an unexpected marriage, childrens' voices, and Sir Shelton sporting his silver bell.

In a captivating story of courage, trust, and faithfulness, will Stormy still be tied in knots or find lasting love by year's end?

Share the joys and sorrows of a mountain community in this swirling saga.

In this collection of true stories titled **Stirrings of The Spirit**, author Sheila Eismann invites you to walk with her family through several valleys en route to some mountain tops as they learned to rely on God in the most harrowing of circumstances.

Have you ever wondered why you were the last one to hear of THE big social event of the year? Well, wonder no longer after reading this e-book titled **Recognize Your Circles**! When volunteering for an organization years ago, author Sheila Eismann was introduced to the concept of "the circles of your life." Since the idea was so beneficial to her, she decided to share it with all of you.

Straight from the Horse's Trough is a humorous read to render assistance to the suburbanite or urbanite who desires to live a healthier lifestyle by growing his or her own food, but is faced with the challenge of a small space in which to do so. This e-book is chock full of how-to steps and includes pictures to remove guesswork from the project.

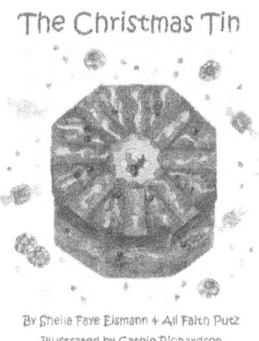

The Christmas Tin is a most delightful read for the young at heart anytime during the year. This endearing book is based upon a true story featuring the older of the two authors when she was a young girl and conveys the timeless message that "love truly is the best gift of all." Children will especially enjoy all of the colorful illustrations contained within this treasure. There's a sugar cookie recipe included in the book and a helpful holiday suggestion for the kiddos to bless someone who's not expecting it at all!

Freedom is Your Destiny! Vietnam Veteran, Dan Eismann, using combat experiences to illustrate spiritual truths, invites you to take a journey with him as he presents a rock-solid strategy for not only fighting your spiritual battles but winning the all-important war. In the midst thereof, the most vital aspect is realizing you can experience freedom and become all that God has destined you to be!

Settle into your special reading spot; grab a cup of tea or your favorite meal. Be stirred as you read and ponder **Poetry Time, Volume One**; allow Sheila's words to encourage and heal.

Everyone can use a little encouragement ~~ a dose of what is beneficial, ethical, and honorable. ***Heart to Heart From God's Word*** provides this for you. Penned with humor and wisdom, the daily tidbits are paired with Bible verses that convey life-changing principles which are designed for readers of all ages transcending cultures and continents. This devotional will challenge you to grow and fulfill your God-given destiny. It can also double as a prayer journal.

A Woman of Substance is a practical, interactive, and entertaining 12-week Bible study penned to help equip you to fulfill your God-given destiny and impact the culture for Jesus Christ at the same time. It can be used as a stand-alone study or devotional and works well in a group setting, too. It is designed for women ages junior high through adult.

ADDITIONAL NOTES & REFLECTIONS

ADDITIONAL NOTES & REFLECTIONS

ADDITIONAL NOTES & REFLECTIONS

ADDITIONAL NOTES & REFLECTIONS

ADDITIONAL NOTES & REFLECTIONS

ADDITIONAL NOTES & REFLECTIONS

ADDITIONAL NOTES & REFLECTIONS

ADDITIONAL NOTES & REFLECTIONS

ADDITIONAL NOTES & REFLECTIONS

ADDITIONAL NOTES & REFLECTIONS

ADDITIONAL NOTES & REFLECTIONS

ADDITIONAL NOTES & REFLECTIONS

ADDITIONAL NOTES & REFLECTIONS

---

[i] Keesee, Ruby, Bible Studies for Women: The Gift of the Word of Knowledge (Caldwell, Idaho, 1990), PP. 1-4.

Keesee, Ruby, Bible Studies for Women: The Gift of the Word of Wisdom (Caldwell, Idaho, 1990), PP. 1-2.

[ii] Keesee, Ruby, Bible Studies for Women: The Gift of Discerning of Spirits, (Caldwell, Idaho, 1990), PP. 1-4.

[iii] Jeremiah 23:28.

[iv] AMG Dictionary – Old Testament, word 5030.

[v] Deuteronomy 18:18.

[vi] Jeremiah 20:8.

[vii] Jeremiah 20:9.

[viii] AMG Dictionary – Old Testament, word 2374.

[ix] AMG Dictionary – Old Testament, word 7200.

[x] Jeremiah 1:7, 9, 11, 12.

[xi] 1 Chronicles 29:29–30.

[xii] 2 Samuel 12:1–4.

[xiii] 2 Samuel 12:5.

[xiv] 2 Samuel 11:2–12:9.

[xv] Luke 1:5, 7, 11, 13, 16–17.

[xvi] 2 Chronicles 24:18–19.

[xvii] Acts 11:27–30.

[xviii] Acts 15:32.

[xix] Acts 13:1–3.

[xx] Jeremiah 1:9–10.

[xxi] House, Paul R. (2008) Note to Jeremiah 1:10. L. T. Dennis (Ex. Ed.), ESV Study Bible, English Standard Version. Wheaton, Ill.: Crossway Bibles.

[xxii] 1 Thessalonians 5:20–21.

[xxiii] 1 Corinthians 14:29–32.

[xxiv] Luke 2:36; Acts 2:17; 21:6.

www.ingramcontent.com/pod-product-compliance
Lightning Source LLC
Chambersburg PA
CBHW080637170426
43200CB00015B/2874